## Student Activity Manual

# Parenting

## Rewards & Responsibilities

McGraw Hill Glencoe

Glencoe

The McGraw-Hill Companies



Send all inquiries to:
Glencoe/McGraw-Hill
4400 Easton Commons
Columbus, OH 43219

13-digit ISBN 978-0-07-869059-4 Student Activity Manual
10-digit ISBN 0-07-869059-5 Student Activity Manual

Printed in the United States of America
9 10 11 QVS 16 15 14

# Contents

## Unit 1: Understanding Parenting

## Chapter 8: Prenatal Development



## Chapter 9: A Healthy Pregnancy



## Chapter 10: Preparing for Baby's Arrival



## Chapter 11: The Birth Process



## Chapter 12: Adapting to Parenthood



# Unit 3: Caring for Children

## Chapter 13: Understanding Infants



## Chapter 14: Caring for Infants



## Chapter 15: Meeting Children's Physical Needs

## Chapter 16: Health and Safety



# Unit 4: Nurturing Children

## Chapter 17: Helping Children Learn



## Chapter 18: Meeting Children's Emotional Needs



## Chapter 19: Helping Children Relate to Others



## Chapter 20: The Value of Play



# Unit 5: Guiding Children

## Chapter 21: Communicating with Children



## Chapter 22: Building Children's Character

Name ______________________ Date ______________ Class ______________

# Study Guide

CHAPTER 1

Parenting and Families

**Directions:** Complete the items that follow in the space provided.

1. Define *parenting*. ______________________________

2. Describe the effects of good parenting on each of the following.

   Individuals: ______________________________

   Families: ______________________________

   Society: ______________________________

3. List five reasons to study parenting.

4. Complete the chart below showing parental concerns in past time periods and those of today. An example has been completed for you.

| Past | Present |
|---|---|
| | Working parents |
| | |
| | |
| | |
| | |

5. List six reasons for forming a family unit.

(Continued on next page)

6. Describe four types of family structures.

7. What is culture?

8. How do families preserve and transmit culture?

9. In the chart below, list the stages in the family life cycle and an event that takes place in each stage.

| The Family Life Cycle | |
|---|---|
| **Stage** | **Event** |
| | |
| | |
| | |
| | |
| | |
| | |
| | |

10. Identify eight ways that people can build strong families. Give an example of each.

Name ______________________ Date ______________ Class ______________



# Preparing for Parenthood

**Directions:** Read each item below. Then answer each item from your own perspective and write your answers in the space provided.

1. Individuals—those who are parents and those who are not—may find themselves in a nurturing role to children. Their experience with children may be brief or last for an extended period of time. When are you around children today? When might you be in a caregiving position in the future?

   Now: ______________________

   Future: ______________________

2. Think of a child that you currently know. Without using his or her name, identify five ways that you could interact with this child to make a difference in his or her life. Then draw one conclusion about how these experiences could help you develop parenting skills for your future.

3. Choose one of the factors that help build strong families at any stage of the life cycle. From the perspective of a parent, list three ways that you could encourage family strength within the context of your chosen factor.

Name ______________________ Date ______________ Class ______________

CHAPTER 1

Parenting and Families

# Parent Interview

**Directions:** Interview two parents—each from a different family. Ask the following questions and summarize the responses in the space provided.

**Parent #1**

1. How is the world different today for your children compared to when you were a child?

_______________________________________________

_______________________________________________

_______________________________________________

2. What is your biggest concern about raising your children in today's world?

_______________________________________________

_______________________________________________

_______________________________________________

3. What do you think makes a strong family?

_______________________________________________

_______________________________________________

_______________________________________________

**Parent #2**

1. How is the world different today for your children compared to when you were a child?

_______________________________________________

_______________________________________________

_______________________________________________

2. What is your biggest concern about raising your children in today's world?

_______________________________________________

_______________________________________________

_______________________________________________

3. What do you think makes a strong family?

_______________________________________________

_______________________________________________

_______________________________________________

**Conclusion**

How do these parents' answers compare with the lists in the textbook? Use another sheet of paper for your answer and attach it to this page.

Name ______________________ Date ______________ Class ______________

# Study Guide

CHAPTER 2

Responsible Parenting

**Directions:** Complete the items that follow in the space provided.

1. Name five common myths about parenting. Contrast these with the realities.

| Parenting Myths | Parenting Realities |
|---|---|
| | |
| | |
| | |
| | |
| | |

2. Name five positive aspects, or rewards, of being a parent.

3. Identify five general responsibilities parents have for their children.

4. List the five needs in Maslow's hierarchy of human needs.

5. Which of the five needs must be met first, before the others? Why?

6. How can parents and caregivers guide children and instill strong values in them?

(Continued on next page)

7. What legal rights do each of the following have in regard to children?

   Parents: ______________________________

   School officials: ______________________________

   Grandparents: ______________________________

8. What is legal emancipation for teens? Under what circumstances might it occur?

9. Parents are legally responsible for providing their children with what five things?

10. Give two examples of circumstances in which the legal responsibilities of parents can be transferred to other adults.

11. What is termination of parental rights?

12. Define child abuse. What are three types of abuse?

13. What is child neglect?

14. If you suspect a child is being abused or neglected, whom should you tell?

15. What types of resources are available to help prevent child abuse?

Name ______________________ Date ______________ Class ______________



# Identify the Needs

**Part I. Directions:** Review the diagram of Maslow's hierarchy of human needs on page 50 of your textbook. Each statement below describes the fulfillment of one need in Maslow's hierarchy. Read each statement carefully and decide which need has been fulfilled. Then write the appropriate number in the blank:

1—Physiological Needs
2—Safety Needs
3—Social Needs
4—Esteem Needs
5—Self-Actualization

______ 1. Tenika accepted the school Junior Science Award. The audience, including her beaming parents and sister, cheered her for her outstanding accomplishment.

______ 2. After feeding and bathing her newborn, Mrs. Angelo put him in his crib for a nap.

______ 3. To get acquainted with their new neighbors, the Emersons invited them to a neighborhood cookout.

______ 4. The Rev. and Mrs. Snow spent five years in the Dominican Republic establishing a school and hospital in a remote village.

______ 5. Mr. and Mrs. Sakahara discussed evacuation procedures from the house with their children. They conduct surprise fire drills at least once a month.

______ 6. Dr. Gomez, a retired psychology professor, does public speaking about equality for all people.

______ 7. Several mothers visit every Thursday morning so their children can play together.

______ 8. When Adam answered the teacher's question correctly, she smiled and said, "You're right!"

______ 9. The public health nurse instructed new parents on childproofing their homes.

______ 10. Lawrence swept the broken glass from the floor before anyone could step on it.

______ 11. Mr. Sawyer keeps a pitcher of filtered water in the refrigerator and encourages his teenagers to drink plenty of water every day.

______ 12. At the end of his swimming lessons, Jesse felt confident about diving into the deep end of the pool.

______ 13. Mr. Kluger gently reprimanded his young son and his son's friend for fighting over a toy. Then he sat down on the floor with them and showed them how to share.

______ 14. When a tornado warning sounded, the Bradley family immediately took shelter in the basement.

______ 15. Tired, Mrs. Yen returned from work and discovered that her daughter had vacuumed the house and started dinner. She told her, "You've made my day!"

______ 16. The artist fulfilled her lifelong dream when she had a one-woman art show in New York City.

**Part II. Directions:** Maslow believed that not everyone reaches the highest level in the hierarchy of needs, which he called *self-actualization*. Do you agree? Why might this be true? Write your answer on a separate sheet of paper and attach it to this activity.

Name ______________________ Date ____________ Class ____________

CHAPTER 2

Responsible Parenting

# Help for Preventing Abuse and Neglect

**Part I. Directions:** Identify three agencies in your community that provide services for families at risk of abuse and neglect. Use reliable Internet or print resources to identify agencies and their services. Write a brief summary in the space provided.

1. Agency Name: ______________________
   Services Provided: ______________________
   ______________________
2. Agency Name: ______________________
   Services Provided: ______________________
   ______________________
3. Agency Name: ______________________
   Services Provided: ______________________
   ______________________

**Part II. Directions:** Select one of the agencies you researched in Part I. Interview a caseworker from this agency, asking the following questions. Summarize the responses in the space provided.

1. In the cases you handle, what factors leading to child abuse or neglect are most often present?
   ______________________
   ______________________
2. How do clients typically find your agency?
   ______________________
   ______________________
3. What steps do you take when you first meet with an individual client or a family?
   ______________________
   ______________________
4. How do you define an at-risk family?
   ______________________
   ______________________
5. What are your goals for a family that is at risk? How do you convey those goals to the family?
   ______________________
   ______________________
6. What are some ways you try to help an at-risk family?
   ______________________
   ______________________

Name ______________________ Date ______________ Class ______________

# Study Guide



**Directions:** Complete the items that follow in the space provided.

1. Self-assessment can help you determine your readiness for parenting. Give four examples of issues that reflect emotional maturity.

2. List five questions that can help you assess your goals in relation to parenting readiness.

3. What increased risks do pregnant teens face?

   What risks do their babies face?

   Besides teen mothers, who else faces increased health risks during pregnancy?

4. There are good reasons and poor reasons to have a baby. Name three of each.

   Good reasons:

   Poor reasons:

(Continued on next page)

5. A healthy relationship between a mother and father provides the best environment for raising a child. Name six factors that contribute to a healthy relationship.

6. What are four financial factors that may affect the decision to have a child?

7. What are three benefits of sexual abstinence besides avoiding pregnancy?

8. Why might some couples postpone parenting or choose not to have children?

9. Educating yourself about parenting can help you determine if it is right for you. What are three ways to do this?

10. Define the following terms.

Self-assessment:

Emotional maturity:

Self-esteem:

Sexually transmitted disease:

Abstinence:

Name ______________________ Date ______________ Class ______________



# Ready or Not?

**Directions:** Read the following situations about couples having a baby or considering having one. Think about whether they are emotionally, financially, and physically ready to become parents. Answer the questions in the space provided.

1. Stacey and Ed have been through some rough times during the five years they have been married. Stacey is hoping to get pregnant within the next year to help smooth their marriage.

   Do you think this couple is ready for a baby? Why or why not?

   ______________________________________________

   ______________________________________________

   What additional problems or conflicts might a baby add to Stacey and Ed's life?

   ______________________________________________

   ______________________________________________

2. Kenyon and Mioni both enjoy children. Mioni works hard at her job to help pay the bills. Kenyon, who has never been very responsible, has had trouble keeping a job for longer than a year at a time.

   Do you think this couple is ready for a baby? Why or why not?

   ______________________________________________

   ______________________________________________

   What advice do you have for Kenyon and Mioni if they do decide to have a baby?

   ______________________________________________

   ______________________________________________

3. The new baby has colic and cries every night from around dinnertime until 10:00 p.m. Isaiah and Afiya calmly take turns holding and trying to comfort her. They have talked to the pediatrician about dealing with colic.

   Do you think this couple is well prepared to handle the responsibilities of parenthood? Why or why not?

   ______________________________________________

   ______________________________________________

   Assess the way Isaiah and Afiya are handling the situation.

   ______________________________________________

   ______________________________________________

(Continued on next page)

4. Reggie and Nicola enjoyed going out with friends before the birth of their twins. Now they look forward to inviting friends over to their house for get-togethers and spending more time with their families.

   Do you think this couple is well prepared to handle the responsibilities of parenthood? Why or why not?

   ___

   ___

   What other activities could Reggie and Nicola do with their twins that would increase their contact with other families?

   ___

   ___

5. Since graduating from college five years ago, Susan and Bryan have concentrated on their careers. They both have well-paying jobs, enabling them to buy a home. Susan recently received a promotion to a position that requires travel during the week. Susan and Bryan have not discussed how their careers may affect their plans for starting a family. Bryan has mentioned, however, that it would be nice to have sons to carry on the family name. Susan believes babies are wonderful, but her career is very important to her right now. She has kept her thoughts and feelings to herself.

   Do you think this couple is ready for a baby? Why or why not?

   ___

   ___

   What questions do they need to discuss about their readiness to become parents?

   ___

   ___

   ___

   ___

6. Joe and Nicole have been married for two years. They recently started discussing the subject of raising a family. Although they both want children, Joe and Nicole want to be ready in every way before a baby arrives.

   What questions do Joe and Nicole need to ask themselves before becoming parents?

   ___

   ___

   ___

   ___

   What advice would you give Joe and Nicole?

   ___

   ___

   ___

   ___

Name ____________________ Date ____________ Class ____________

# Study Guide

CHAPTER 4

Understanding Child Development

**Directions:** Complete the items that follow in the space provided.

1. Define the following terms.

   Development: ____________________

   Infancy: ____________________

   Toddler: ____________________

   Preschooler: ____________________

   Middle childhood: ____________________

   Early adolescence: ____________________

   Late adolescence: ____________________

   Puberty: ____________________

   Heredity: ____________________

   Environment: ____________________

   Theory: ____________________

   Neurons: ____________________

   Synapses: ____________________

   Chromosomes: ____________________

   Gene: ____________________

2. Name and describe the five areas in which children develop.

(Continued on next page)

3. Explain four basic principles of child development.

________________________________________
________________________________________
________________________________________
________________________________________
________________________________________
________________________________________
________________________________________
________________________________________

4. Development is influenced by ____________________ and ____________________.
Describe how each of these two factors affects development.

________________________________________
________________________________________
________________________________________
________________________________________
________________________________________
________________________________________

5. Fill in the chart below by identifying the theorist who developed each child development theory.

| Theorist | Description of Child Development Theory |
|---|---|
| | Children build knowledge by actively participating in the learning process. |
| | Children develop at their own rate, based on an "inner timetable" determined by heredity. |
| | Children learn best by memorizing facts. Teachers should set clear objectives and provide positive reinforcement. |
| | Children learn by interacting with their environment. They go through four stages of cognitive development. |
| | Children learn by socializing with adults and more capable peers. Intellectual development is limited to certain skills at any given age. |
| | Children learn through a four-step process of watching and imitating others. |
| | Children need to resolve a particular crisis at each stage of development before they can move on to the next stage. |
| | Children develop by interacting with four different types of environments: microsystem, mesosystem, exosystem, and macrosystem. |
| | Morally, people progress from obeying authority to meeting society's expectations, and finally to truly caring about others. |
| | This theorist developed theories of moral development based on interviews with inner city children. |

Name ______________________ Date ______________ Class ______________



# Stages of Development

**Directions:** In the chart below, fill in examples of development in each area at each stage of childhood.

| Development Stage | Physical Development | Intellectual Development | Emotional, Social, and Moral Development |
|---|---|---|---|
| Infancy | | | |
| Toddler Stage | | | |
| Preschool Stage | | | |
| Middle Childhood | | | |
| Early Adolescence | | | |
| Late Adolescence | | | |

Name ______________________ Date ____________ Class ____________

CHAPTER 4

Understanding Child Development

# Heredity and Environment

**Directions:** Two general factors influence development—heredity and environment. As you read the following situations, think about the specific factors that *may* have influenced these people to accomplish what they did. In the space provided, identify possible ways in which heredity and environment may have contributed to each person's behavior.

1. John is six feet tall and slender. When he was in grade school and junior high, he often shot hoops in his driveway with his older brothers. Now John is a starter on the high school basketball team.

   Heredity: ______________________

   Environment: ______________________

   Which do you think had more influence in John's accomplishment? Why? ______________________

2. Srirath was interested in science as a child. She enjoyed biology lab and chemistry in high school. Although her parents could not afford to send her to college, she studied hard and talked with her school counselor about applying for scholarships. She was awarded a scholarship for undergraduate school and saved enough money to go to veterinary school. She is now a veterinarian.

   Heredity: ______________________

   Environment: ______________________

   Which do you think had more influence in Srirath's accomplishment? Why? ______________________

Name ______________________ Date ____________ Class ____________

# Study Guide

CHAPTER 5

Effective Parenting Skills

**Directions:** Complete the items that follow in the space provided.

1. Name four personal management skills. Describe how each can help parents be more effective.

| Management Skill | How It Can Help Parents |
|---|---|
| | |
| | |
| | |
| | |

2. What does prioritizing mean?

3. What is a goal? How can long-term goals and short-term goals work together?

4. What is a resource? Name three kinds of resources for parenting.

5. What are the four major steps in the management process?

6. What are some activities you may need to do in the second phase of the management process?

7. What are the six steps in the decision-making process?

8. When using the *practical reasoning* process, what are four different angles from which you can look at a situation?

(Continued on next page)

9. Name three interpersonal skills important for parents, and tell why each is important.

10. What are the two main goals of conflict resolution?

11. Define negotiation, and explain how a mediator might help in a negotiation.

12. What are some guidelines for settling a conflict?

13. List six personal qualities that make for successful parenting.

14. Name and describe the three basic parenting styles.

15. List several ways parents can learn more about building parenting skills.

# The Right Stuff

**Directions:** The qualities listed below are helpful to parents, as well as to others. Most people have these qualities to some degree, but most people also have room for improvement. Complete the chart by giving at least one example of how you show each quality in your life right now. Then identify at least one step you could take to develop this quality further.

| | How I Show This Quality Now | How I Could Develop This Quality Further |
|---|---|---|
| Patience | | |
| Confidence | | |
| Realistic Expectations | | |
| Positive Attitude | | |
| Sense of Humor | | |
| Sensitivity | | |

Name ______________________ Date ____________ Class ____________

CHAPTER 5

Effective Parenting Skills

# Analyzing Parenting Styles

**Directions:** Fill in the chart below explaining how parents with the three basic parenting styles might react in each situation described. Remember to consider how the three styles differ in terms of:

- How rules are established.
- What parents expect once rules are established.
- How much freedom children have to make their own decisions.

| Situation | Authoritarian | Authoritative | Permissive |
|---|---|---|---|
| 1. A four-year-old thinks he should be able to stay up as late as the adults in the family, who go to bed around 11:00 p.m. on weeknights. | | | |
| 2. A seven-year-old complains that she does not like the healthful foods her parent packs in her school lunchbox. The parent suspects that the child throws the packed lunch away and buys candy. | | | |
| 3. A ten-year-old's parents want him to take a shower in the evening to save time in the morning. The child would rather play video games after his homework is done, then go to bed without showering. | | | |

Name ______________________ Date ______________ Class ______________



# Making a Decision

**Directions:** Read the situation below, then complete the items that follow.

Eight-year-old Felix wants to take piano lessons. His parents would like to encourage his interest in music, but they have some reservations. The family does not own a piano and does not have the money to buy one. Felix's parents also wonder how to find a skilled, affordable piano teacher.

1. Think of two possible ways to provide Felix with a piano to practice on. Identify pros and cons of each option.

| Possible Options | Pros | Cons |
| --- | --- | --- |
| | | |
| | | |

2. Which of the options above would you choose? Why? ______________________

3. Name three sources of advice that might help Felix's parents find a suitable piano teacher.

4. If Felix's parents decide to allow Felix to take piano lessons, when do you think they should evaluate their decision? What should they look for?

5. If Felix's parents decide not to allow him to take piano lessons, what other alternatives might they offer him that would allow him to pursue his interest in music?

Name ______________________ Date ______________ Class ______________

CHAPTER 5

Effective Parenting Skills

# Resolving Conflicts

**Directions:** In each of the situations below, the way family members chose to handle a conflict created problems. Read each situation and identify the negative outcomes that resulted. Then suggest how the participants could have found a better way to resolve their conflict.

1. The Smith's four-year-old wandered into the next door neighbor's yard and ran across the flower bed. The neighbor yelled at Mrs. Smith and stormed into the house. Mrs. Smith vowed never to speak to her again.

   Negative outcome: ______________________________

   ______________________________

   Better solution: ______________________________

   ______________________________

2. Six-year-old Darin wanted to go to the park to play. Eight-year-old Riley wanted to go to the zoo instead. Their father told both boys their ideas were poor choices and he'd decide what to do for the afternoon.

   Negative outcome: ______________________________

   ______________________________

   Better solution: ______________________________

   ______________________________

3. Mr. and Mrs. Washington were having disagreements about their finances. He thought it was a great time to buy a new car. She said they couldn't afford the car payments and that he was always irresponsible about money. They argued about it for days.

   Negative outcome: ______________________________

   ______________________________

   Better solution: ______________________________

   ______________________________

   ______________________________

4. Although Jennifer's curfew was usually 11 p.m., she asked permission to go to a concert and stay out until 1 a.m. on Saturday. Mrs. Johnson said Jennifer could go to the concert if she came home by midnight. Jennifer agreed just so she could go to the concert. Then she stayed out until 1 a.m. like she wanted to.

   Negative outcome: ______________________________

   ______________________________

   Better solution: ______________________________

   ______________________________

   ______________________________

Name ____________________ Date ____________ Class ____________

# Study Guide

CHAPTER 6

Teens and Parenting

**Directions:** Complete the items that follow in the space provided.

1. Name four internal pressures that contribute to teen pregnancy.

2. Name three sources of external pressure on teens that can contribute to teen pregnancy.

3. Name five medical risks that affect teen mothers more than adult mothers.

4. What are three medical risks to the baby of a teen mother?

5. In addition to health risks, what are four other challenges teen parents face?

6. Name three outcomes that children of teen parents are more likely to face than children of adult parents.

7. Besides teen parents and their children, name two other groups of people affected by teen parenthood and describe the effects on each.

8. Describe three parenthood options available to teens who have a baby.

9. Name four types of adoption.

(Continued on next page)

10. Explain the rights and responsibilities of teen parents.

11. Name seven sources of support and advice for teen parents.

12. Define the following terms.

Prenatal care:

Miscarriage:

Stillbirth:

Premature birth:

Low birth weight:

Human immunodeficiency virus:

Paternity:

Adoption:

Closed adoption:

Open adoption:

Semi-open adoption:

In-family adoption:

Name ______________________ Date ______________ Class ______________



# Tackling Tough Challenges

**Directions:** Read the situations below. Answer the questions using practical reasoning to help the people in the situations examine their problems and look at the situation from different angles.

1. Seventeen-year-old Hannah is having difficulty coping with her parents' divorce. She is glad she has a boyfriend to talk with and to keep her mind off her family troubles. Lately, Hannah has been thinking about having a baby. She thinks that having a baby would bring more meaning to her life.

   What are the circumstances surrounding the decision? ______________________________

   What results does Hannah want? ______________________________

   Besides having a baby, what options does Hannah have to solve her problem of coping with the divorce?

   ______________________________

   What are the consequences of the action she is considering? ______________________________

2. Barb and Patrick, age 18, have been dating since they were sophomores in high school. They have strong feelings for each other but have remained true to their commitment not to have sex before marriage. However, their friends are teasing them about abstinence.

   What circumstances are affecting their commitment? ______________________________

   How can Barb and Patrick keep their commitment? ______________________________

(Continued on next page)

3. Tim's girlfriend, Holly, just told him he is going to be a father in six months. He and Holly believe they are in love, but they were planning to go to college next year and get married after they both graduated.

   Name three options they have concerning their relationship and the baby.

   ______________________________

   ______________________________

   ______________________________

   What responsibilities does Tim have no matter which option they choose for the baby?

   ______________________________

   ______________________________

   ______________________________

   Whom could they turn to for guidance and support? ______________________________

   ______________________________

   ______________________________

   What other aspects of their lives do they need to discuss? ______________________________

   ______________________________

   ______________________________

4. Lamar and Catera have been dating for several months. He is pressuring her to have sex with him. Although Catera cares for Lamar, she does not want to have sex.

   What can Catera say to him? ______________________________

   ______________________________

   ______________________________

   ______________________________

   What results might happen if Catera initates an open conversation about sex and explains her feelings?

   ______________________________

   ______________________________

   ______________________________

   How might they avoid the temptation? ______________________________

   ______________________________

   ______________________________

Name ______________________ Date ____________ Class ____________

# Study Guide

CHAPTER 7

Planning a Family

**Directions:** Complete the items that follow in the space provided.

1. Identify three reasons for planning a family, rather than leaving parenthood to chance.

2. Name at least four factors couples need to discuss when planning a family.

3. Name five steps potential parents should take to prepare physically for a healthy pregnancy and parenthood.

4. Define the following reproductive terms:

   Ovaries: ______________________

   Uterus, or womb: ______________________

   Ova: ______________________

   Ovulation: ______________________

   Fallopian tubes: ______________________

   Testes: ______________________

   Sperm: ______________________

   Conception: ______________________

(Continued on next page)

5. Briefly explain how conception occurs.

6. What factors influence a couple's decision about contraceptives?

7. What method of contraception is 100% effective?

8. Explain how fraternal and identical twins are formed.

9. What are some causes of infertility?

10. What are chromosomes? How many chromosomes are in each ovum and sperm? How many chromosomes are in all the other cells of the human body?

11. How are traits passed from parents to children?

12. What are two alternatives to biological parenthood? What is the difference between the two?

13. What are some reasons couples might choose to adopt a child?

Name ______________________ Date ______________ Class ______________



# Advice from an Expert

**Directions:** Dr. Susan Ling, a noted obstetrician/gynecologist, is on a radio talk show addressing myths and facts about human reproduction. Answer the questions below as you imagine she would.

1. I've heard that conception takes place in the uterus. Is that correct?

2. Isn't it true that sperm die after 18 hours?

3. Since I've never had a period, I can't get pregnant, right?

4. My wife and I have been trying to conceive a child for a year. Does that mean we can't ever have children?

5. Our child looks more like me than my wife. Does that mean all his genes came from me?

6. My friend just had a boy and a girl. She says they are fraternal twins. I thought twins had to be the same sex. Can you explain this to me?

Name ______________________ Date ____________ Class ____________

CHAPTER 7

Planning a Family

# Adoption

**Part I. Directions:** Identify three agencies in your community that provide adoption services. Use the Internet or print resources to identify agencies and their services. Write a brief summary in the space provided.

Agency Name: ______________________

Services Provided: ______________________

______________________

______________________

______________________

Agency Name: ______________________

Services Provided: ______________________

______________________

______________________

______________________

Agency Name: ______________________

Services Provided: ______________________

______________________

______________________

______________________

**Part II. Directions:** Select one of the agencies you researched in Part I and interview a caseworker from this agency. Write your interview responses to the following questions on a separate sheet of paper and attach it to this activity.

1. What steps does a woman who wants to place her baby for adoption take?
2. What counseling do you offer her?
3. How is a prospective adoptive parent screened?
4. What sources are available for locating children available for adoption?
5. What are the costs of adopting a baby?
6. How long does the adoption process usually take?
7. What steps do adoptive parents take to make the adoption final?
8. What steps does a person take to be eligible to care for foster children?

Name ______________________ Date ____________ Class ____________

# Study Guide

CHAPTER 8

Prenatal Development

**Directions:** Complete the items that follow in the space provided.

1. A pregnancy is divided into three time periods called ______________________. Each lasts ______________________.
2. What are the three stages of prenatal development? What happens at the beginning of each stage?

______________________

3. In the blanks below, write *1*, *2*, or *3* for the trimester in which each development occurs in the unborn baby.

   _____ The heart begins to pump.
   _____ Fat tissue and body hair begin to form.
   _____ The baby may suck his or her thumb.
   _____ The senses develop as nerve cells make connections with the brain.
   _____ The baby sleeps and may dream.
   _____ Lungs are almost fully developed.
   _____ The baby grows from a few cells to about three inches long.
   _____ The baby turns his or her head downward, readying for birth.
   _____ The eyes, ears, mouth, and nostrils begin to form.
   _____ The mother begins to feel the baby move around and kick.
   _____ The liver begins to produce bile and the kidneys to produce urine.
   _____ Eyes open and close for the first time.

4. What is the function of amniotic fluid?

______________________

5. Explain how the placenta and umbilical cord support the developing baby.

______________________

6. What is a miscarriage?

______________________

(Continued on next page)

7. What is a stillbirth? How often does it occur?

8. Name three risk factors that may increase the chance of miscarriage.

9. What is an ectopic pregnancy? What is done when an ectopic pregnancy occurs?

10. Explain how genetic birth defects can occur.

11. Name several environmental causes of birth defects.

12. A premature birth occurs when a baby is born before the ____________ week of pregnancy. What problems do the tiniest babies typically face?

13. Name three types of prenatal tests and briefly explain how each is done.

14. Offer four suggestions for coping with the loss of a pregnancy.

# Letters to a Friend

**Directions:** Your friends Jane and Rick, a 22-year-old married couple, have moved to another state. You have agreed to keep in touch with letters or e-mail. Read their letters and write your responses in the space provided. Be sure to provide information that will help Jane and Rick with their questions and concerns.

**March 4.** Guess what! We're going to have a baby! We're very excited. The doctor says it's an embryo now, but we always hear people talking about a fetus. What's the difference? We're doing well and hope you are too. Love, Jane and Rick

______________________________

______________________________

______________________________

______________________________

______________________________

______________________________

**March 28.** Thanks for your letter. We're having a good time and trying to figure out how to be good parents. We're cutting down a little on cigarettes. We figure we might as well change our habits now so we can set the child a good example after the birth. Love, Jane and Rick

______________________________

______________________________

______________________________

______________________________

______________________________

______________________________

**April 19.** The doctors and nurses seem to want to do test after test. They check Jane's blood and urine (what's that about?) and they're planning an ultrasound. We can't decide whether to avoid all tests as dangerous or take every test possible. What would you do? Love, Jane and Rick

______________________________

______________________________

______________________________

______________________________

______________________________

______________________________

(Continued on next page)

Letters to a Friend (continued)

**April 26.** So why isn't the baby kicking? Aren't you supposed to feel a baby kicking by now? We're in the fourth month of pregnancy already. Do you suppose something might be wrong? How can we tell whether to worry? Love, Jane and Rick

**May 12.** We're rearranging the apartment to get ready for the baby, and we've been hanging pictures. Rick keeps reminding me not to move furniture or be very active. We've heard that can cause a miscarriage. The doctor says everything is going well. Love, Jane and Rick

**May 20.** It's a boy! When I put my hand on Jane's belly we can both feel him kicking. He must be growing fast. Everyone says Jane's eating for two, but how does her eating help the baby grow? Love, Jane and Rick

**July 5.** We haven't chosen a name yet, but we talk about him all the time. Do you think he can hear us? We'd better watch what we say! Do you suppose he heard last night's fireworks? Love, Jane and Rick

Name ______________________ Date ______________ Class ______________

# Study Guide

CHAPTER 9

A Healthy Pregnancy

**Directions:** Complete the items that follow in the space provided.

1. List several early signs of pregnancy.

2. How is a pregnancy most reliably detected?

3. What is prenatal care? What are the benefits of receiving such care?

4. Describe each of the following potential health risks.

   Rh factor: ______________________

   Preeclampsia: ______________________

   Gestational diabetes: ______________________

5. What are four physical discomforts a pregnant woman might experience? Name one way to cope with each.

(Continued on next page)

6. Describe the emotional changes a woman may experience during pregnancy.

7. Offer five suggestions for managing stress during pregnancy.

8. Summarize recommendations for pregnant women regarding rest and exercise.

9. How do a woman's calorie needs typically change during pregnancy?

10. What vitamin is especially important during pregnancy? Why?

11. What is anemia? What risks does it create for the developing baby? How can it be prevented?

12. Why should a pregnant woman avoid eating raw or undercooked meat?

13. Name five types of health hazards during pregnancy. What are a few of the complications for unborn babies exposed to these hazards?

Name ______________________ Date ______________ Class ______________



# Plan the Meals

**Directions:** Your older sister, who is pregnant, will be visiting with you one full day next week. You will be preparing her meals and snacks for the day. In the chart below, plan the day's menu, listing the foods you will serve and the amounts. Be sure the amounts for each food group add up to the recommended daily total. When you have completed your menu, answer the questions that follow.

| | Grain Group | Vegetable Group | Fruit Group | Milk Group | Meat & Beans Group |
|---|---|---|---|---|---|
| **Recommended amounts** | 7 to 8 ounces | 3 cups | 2 cups | 3 cups | 6 to 6.5 ounces |
| **Breakfast** | | | | | |
| **Snack** | | | | | |
| **Lunch** | | | | | |
| **Snack** | | | | | |
| **Dinner** | | | | | |
| **Snack** | | | | | |
| **Total amounts** | | | | | |

(Continued on next page)

## Plan the Meals (continued)

1. List the foods in your menu that supply the following nutrients.

   Vitamin A: ______

   B vitamins: ______

   Vitamin C: ______

   Vitamin D: ______

   Vitamin E: ______

   Calcium: ______

   Iron: ______

2. Explain how your menu addresses food safety for a pregnant woman. For example, will some of the foods on your menu require special care in shopping or preparation? What foods did you avoid in your menu and why?

3. Your sister has been experiencing a common discomfort of pregnancy—constipation. Which foods and beverages in your menu plan can help relieve this discomfort?

4. Since the time that you created your menu plan, your sister has been told by her physician that she needs to increase her daily calorie intake by 300 calories. Explain how you could alter your existing meal plan to allow for this increase in calories.

# Prenatal Care Pays Off

**Part I. Directions:** The following statements describe the behavior of pregnant women. If you think the woman is doing a healthful thing, write a (+) in the space provided. If you think her behavior could be harmful, write a (0) in the space.

_____ 1. Angela drinks diet cola during her pregnancy so she won't gain more than 16 pounds.

_____ 2. Paula likes to try new sports, but she decided to postpone water skiing until after her baby is born.

_____ 3. Jasmine takes her prescribed vitamin supplements daily and eats a nutritious diet.

_____ 4. Samantha is experiencing constipation. Without consulting her doctor, she decided to try a laxative.

_____ 5. Lisa quit smoking when she learned she was pregnant, but doesn't leave the room when her husband or friends smoke.

_____ 6. Soraya takes daily naps or finds time to sit down and read a book.

_____ 7. Colleen's hamburger was cooked very rare, but she ate it anyway.

_____ 8. Laura is allergic to cats. She borrowed her friend's allergy medication until her next doctor's visit.

_____ 9. Meta waited six months after her measles vaccine before becoming pregnant.

_____ 10. Jamie suspected she had chlamydia. Ignoring her embarrassment, she notified her doctor.

_____ 11. Kelly used to watch horror movies that made her nervous and kept her awake. Since becoming pregnant, she has switched to watching comedy.

_____ 12. Hiroyo purchased a pair of flat shoes one size larger than her usual shoe size.

_____ 13. To avoid looking pregnant, Abby wears tight clothes to hold in her abdomen.

**Part II. Directions:** All the women in Part I will be taking a six-session class on "Healthy Pregnancy." You are helping to plan one of the sessions. You hope to reinforce the women's healthy practices and help them correct their unhealthy practices. Fill in the following information.

Choose a topic for your session:

______________________________________________

Main points you will present in the session:

______________________________________________

______________________________________________

______________________________________________

______________________________________________

Which of the women in the class are most in need of the information in this session?

______________________________________________

Name ______________________ Date ______________ Class ______________

CHAPTER 9

A Healthy Pregnancy

# Mom AND Dad

**Part I. Directions:** Although the mother carries the baby in her uterus, the father plays an important role during the pregnancy, too. Complete the items below to describe some ways the father can be involved during this time.

1. How can the father be involved with the mother's medical care?

   Choice of health care provider: ______________________

   Prenatal examinations: ______________________

   Understanding pregnancy: ______________________

2. How can the father support the mother's physical self-care?

   Rest: ______________________

   Exercise: ______________________

   Diet: ______________________

   Stress: ______________________

   Clothing: ______________________

   Drugs, alcohol, and tobacco: ______________________

3. How can the father support the mother in coping with possible physical and emotional changes?

   Weight gain: ______________________

   Nausea: ______________________

   Trouble sleeping: ______________________

   Mood swings: ______________________

   Depression: ______________________

**Part II. Directions:** Fathers have emotions during pregnancy, too. Complete the items below to suggest emotions the father may feel and ways the couple can help him cope.

1. Why might the father feel left out? ______________________

   ______________________

2. What can help the father feel less left out? ______________________

   ______________________

3. Why might the father feel anxious? ______________________

   ______________________

4. What can help the father feel less anxious? ______________________

   ______________________

Name ______________________ Date ____________ Class ____________

# Study Guide



**Directions:** Complete the items that follow in the space provided.

1. How might parents-to-be prepare the children they already have for the arrival of a new baby?

2. What is the main advantage of a hospital birth? Of a birthing center?

3. Is home birth an option for all pregnant women? Explain.

4. What is prepared childbirth? What do couples learn at prepared childbirth classes?

5. What is a birth plan? What might it include?

6. What expenses must expectant parents consider in relation to the baby's birth and later on?

(Continued on next page)

7. List several options parents might have for child care.

8. What are some considerations in choosing a doctor for a baby?

9. List some advantages of breast-feeding and bottle-feeding.

10. Name three types of diapers available to parents.

11. Name factors parents should think about when selecting the following.

Crib:

Baby clothes:

Infant car seat:

12. Is it necessary for a newborn to have toys? Why or why not?

13. In addition to preparing the baby's room, what are some tasks that the expectant parents can do before the delivery date to make their trip to the birthing facility and their return home go smoothly?

Name ______________________ Date ____________ Class ____________



# Someone New in the Family!

**Directions:** At a library or bookstore, select two books designed for parents to read with children about a new baby brother or sister. For each book, provide the information listed.

**Book #1** Title: ______________________

Author: ______________________

Age group book is intended for: ______________________

Summary of the book: ______________________

Do you think the text of the book is well written and interesting? Why or why not? ______________________

Does this book provide accurate information? Explain. ______________________

Do you think children would find the illustrations appealing? Why or why not? ______________________

Do you feel this book is appropriate for the intended age group? Why or why not? ______________________

What special features, if any, add to this book's appeal? ______________________

Overall, would you recommend this book to parents? Why or why not? ______________________

(Continued on next page)

## Someone New in the Family! (continued)

**Book #2** Title: ____________________

Author: ____________________

Age group book is intended for: ____________________

Summary of the book: ____________________

Do you think the text of the book is well written and interesting? Why or why not? ____________________

Does this book provide accurate information? Explain. ____________________

Do you think children would find the illustrations appealing? Why or why not? ____________________

Do you feel this book is appropriate for the intended age group? Why or why not? ____________________

What special features, if any, add to this book's appeal? ____________________

Overall, would you recommend this book to parents? Why or why not? ____________________

Name ______________________ Date ______________ Class ______________



# What Will You Say?

**Directions:** Listed below are things different people might say to a pregnant woman and her husband as they prepare for the birth of their second child. Imagine that you are one of the expectant parents. Read each quotation and respond to the questions that follow.

**Older neighbor woman:** "What do you mean, birthing center? It doesn't sound safe. I had my babies at a hospital and so should you."

Why do you suppose she says it? ______________________

How do you feel when she says it? ______________________

What will you say in response? ______________________

**Married male friend:** "You are so lucky. We've been trying and trying to have a child, and now you're going to have two. It doesn't seem fair."

Why do you suppose he says it? ______________________

How do you feel when he says it? ______________________

What will you say in response? ______________________

**Your three-year-old son:** "I don't want you to have a baby. I'm your baby."

Why do you suppose he says it? ______________________

How do you feel when he says it? ______________________

What will you say in response? ______________________

(Continued on next page)

## What Will You Say? (continued)

**Female cousin:** "Are you going to breast-feed or bottle-feed? I wouldn't know how to choose."

Why do you suppose she says it? ______________________________

______________________________

How do you feel when she says it? ______________________________

______________________________

What will you say in response? ______________________________

______________________________

______________________________

**Aunt and uncle:** "Here's our old crib. This family has been using it for generations."

Why do you suppose they say it? ______________________________

______________________________

How do you feel when they say it? ______________________________

______________________________

What will you say in response? ______________________________

______________________________

______________________________

______________________________

**Your coworkers:** "We'd like to give you a baby shower. What kinds of things would you like?"

Why do you suppose they say it? ______________________________

______________________________

How do you feel when they say it? ______________________________

______________________________

What will you say in response? ______________________________

______________________________

______________________________

______________________________

**Your parents (the new grandparents):** "We'd like to help you out with a gift of diaper service, or else cloth or disposable diapers. Do you know which you plan to use?"

Why do you suppose they say it? ______________________________

______________________________

How do you feel when they say it? ______________________________

______________________________

What will you say in response? ______________________________

______________________________

______________________________

______________________________

Name ______________________ Date ______________ Class ______________

# Study Guide



**Directions:** Complete the items that follow in the space provided.

1. Explain three indicators that signal the beginning of labor.

2. Describe the characteristics of false labor contractions.

3. Briefly summarize what happens in each of the three stages of labor.

4. Describe what happens in each phase of the first stage of labor.

   Early labor: ______________________

   Active labor: ______________________

   Transition: ______________________

5. List some factors that can reduce the discomfort and pain a woman experiences during the birth process.

6. Describe how the baby travels through the birth canal and emerges in a typical birth.

7. How long does the third stage of labor usually take?

(Continued on next page)

8. What is a cesarean delivery? Give an example of when it might be necessary.

9. Describe the physical characteristics of newborns.

10. What is bonding?

11. Name four postnatal procedures done on the baby almost immediately.

12. What postnatal care does the mother receive?

13. Describe neonatal intensive care.

14. What are three possible arrangements for where the baby stays while in the hospital?

15. What are some advantages of a rooming-in arrangement after the baby's birth?

Name ______________________ Date ______________ Class ______________



# Thoughts and Feelings

**Directions:** Imagine the emotional roller coaster that a new mother and father might experience when their baby is born. Respond to the following items in the space provided.

1. The mother's water breaks, signaling the beginning of labor. What might she think and feel?

2. The father in the birthing room watches his wife experience the pain of labor. What might he think and feel?

3. The parents see the new baby. Instead of picture-perfect, it looks blotchy and cross-eyed. What might they think and feel?

4. The mother holds the newborn baby on her stomach while the father talks to the baby. What might they think and feel?

5. The new parents get home with the baby. They have taken classes but they have never been alone with a baby before. What might they think and feel?

Name ____________________ Date ____________ Class ____________



# Decisions, Decisions

**Directions:** During and after labor, the mother faces many decisions. Imagine yourself in each of the following situations, then respond to the items in order to reason your way to a decision.

1. It's the middle of the night and I don't know if this is false labor or real. What should I do?
   Factors to consider: ____________________
   ____________________
   Possible decision: ____________________
   ____________________
   Reason(s) for that decision: ____________________
   ____________________

2. Do I want to be given pain-relieving medication during labor? If so, what type of medication?
   Factors to consider: ____________________
   ____________________
   Possible decision: ____________________
   ____________________
   Reason(s) for that decision: ____________________
   ____________________

3. During the hospital stay, do I want the baby in the room with me or just brought in to visit and nurse?
   Factors to consider: ____________________
   ____________________
   Possible decision: ____________________
   ____________________
   Reason(s) for that decision: ____________________
   ____________________

4. I've been told I can go home after one day or stay in the hospital two days. Which shall I do?
   Factors to consider: ____________________
   ____________________
   Possible decision: ____________________
   ____________________
   Reason(s) for that decision: ____________________
   ____________________

Name ______________________ Date ______________ Class ______________

## Study Guide

CHAPTER 12

Adapting to Parenthood

**Directions:** Complete the items that follow in the space provided.

1. Describe some physical changes that occur in new mothers.

2. Describe nutrition guidelines for a new mother.

3. When is a postnatal checkup given? What does it include?

4. What are the "baby blues"? What causes them?

5. What is postpartum depression? How does it differ from the baby blues?

6. Give three examples of common challenges new parents face.

(Continued on next page)

7. Name four management strategies that can help new parents handle these challenges.

8. What is a support system? Who might be included in a support system? Give some examples of how it might work.

9. What are four ways couples can help each other adjust to their new roles and strengthen their own relationship?

10. How can good communication skills help new parents?

11. Name three ways parents can help their children adjust to a new baby in the family.

12. What special challenges might single parents face?

13. Name some special concerns that adoptive parents might face.

Name ______________________ Date ______________ Class ______________



# Where to Turn for Help

**Directions:** If something is wrong, the first step in correcting it is identifying the problem. The second and third steps are deciding what kind of help is needed and where to turn for help. For each of the following problems, indicate what kinds of help the couple might want from their support system and at least three possible sources of help.

| Problem | Kind of Help Needed | Sources of Help |
|---|---|---|
| The baby has cried much of the night for the past three nights. Both parents are exhausted and need some sleep. | | |
| The new parents have not been alone together since the baby was born. They'd like to spend some quality time—just the two of them. | | |
| The new mother is unsure of her skills as a parent. She's worried that she is not bathing and feeding her newborn correctly. | | |
| The couple had always been able to discuss their differences before. However, since the baby was born, the new mother and father find themselves arguing often. | | |

(Continued on next page)

| Problem | Kind of Help Needed | Sources of Help |
|---|---|---|
| Although the parents have tried to involve the new baby's older brother and pay specific attention to him, he continues to act jealous of the baby. The parents are afraid he will try to harm the newborn. | | |
| A single mom finds herself feeling alone and isolated. She cries often. | | |
| A couple has just adopted a two-year-old from a different country. They have many questions about how to make the child a part of their family. | | |

Name ______________________ Date ____________ Class ____________



# What Would You Do?

**Directions:** Read the following situations and answer the questions.

**Jim's Situation**

Jim is overwhelmed with his new role as a father. Now that his wife, Kelly, is so busy caring for their baby, Jim feels left out of her life. He does not feel as if he is part of their baby daughter's daily routine either. And on top of everything else, he is worried about their finances now that they have a child.

1. How can Jim and his wife, Kelly, remain close and build on their relationship when the new baby takes so much time and energy?

2. How can he become more involved with his new daughter?

3. What steps can Jim take to alleviate his financial worries?

**Miranda's Situation**

Miranda's five-year-old daughter, Shawna, is driving her crazy. Since the birth of her baby brother, Shawna seems to have a different personality. She resorts to tantrums when she doesn't get her way. She says she hates the new baby. She cries to be rocked at night before bedtime.

4. Is Shawna's behavior something to be concerned about? Explain.

(Continued on next page)

## What Would You Do? (continued)

5. How should Miranda respond to Shawna's behavior?

### The Grandparents' Situation

Parents and siblings are not the only ones adjusting to the new family member. Grandparents have a new role to play, too. If this baby is their first grandchild, they may even be overwhelmed.

6. What positive feelings and thoughts might grandparents experience when the new baby arrives? What negative feelings and thoughts might they have?

7. If the grandparents live nearby, how can they be of help? How can they benefit from being involved in the baby's life? What warnings would you offer to parents in asking the grandparents for help?

8. If grandparents live far away, how can the new parents involve them in the new baby's life?

Name ______________________ Date ______________ Class ______________

# Study Guide

CHAPTER 13

Understanding Infants

**Directions:** Complete the items that follow in the space provided.

1. Define *development*. How does development differ from growth?

2. Describe changes in growth and proportion in the first year of life.

3. What is "failure to thrive"? Why do some babies experience this problem?

4. What are reflexes? What does their presence at birth indicate?

5. Name the five senses. Describe the development of one.

6. Give an example of an infant's large motor skill for each age listed below.
   3–4 months: ______________
   5–6 months: ______________
   7–8 months: ______________
   9–10 months: ______________
   11–12 months: ______________

7. How is sensory stimulation related to brain development and learning?

(Continued on next page)

8. Explain Piaget's first four stages of a child's sensorimotor development.

| Stage | Age | Learning/Development |
|---|---|---|
| Stage 1 | | |
| Stage 2 | | |
| Stage 3 | | |
| Stage 4 | | |

9. What are infants' first two emotional states? What other emotions do they express by about one year of age?

10. What are the key tasks of emotional development in an infant?

11. What is attachment behavior? Why is it important for a child's emotional and social development?

12. Summarize social development in the first year. How can parents help babies develop their social skills?

13. In what way do infants develop morally?

Name ________________________ Date ______________ Class ______________



# How Well Do You Understand Infants?

**Directions:** Answer the questions about the following situations.

1. Kerry and her friend Samantha both gave birth to their first child within a few days of each other. Kerry has noticed that Samantha's baby is doing activities sooner than her baby. She is worried that something is wrong with her child. What advice would you give to Kerry?

2. You and your spouse have agreed to watch your friends' six-month-old baby for an evening. You get out some infant toys and a few simple books with colorful photos. Your spouse thinks you are silly for wanting to read to a baby. How do you explain that reading to babies is a good idea?

3. Mariah and Amad's first child was easygoing as an infant. They could take him in his infant carrier when they went to family gatherings and friends' homes. However, their second child usually cries and becomes upset around a large group of people. What advice would you give to Mariah and Amad for handling this?

4. Ramon's daughter, Elisa, is eight months old. His son Mateo, who is three years old, sometimes gets rough with his little sister, making her cry. How can Ramon help Mateo interact appropriately with Elisa?

Name ______________________ Date ____________ Class ____________

CHAPTER 13

Understanding Infants

# First Things First

**Directions:** Infants must accomplish simpler skills before they can develop more advanced skills. In each group of motor skills below, mark the order in which an infant learns to do them. Mark the first skill learned with a *1*, the second with a *2*, and so on. Then choose one skill in each group and describe a way to encourage a child who is beginning to develop that skill.

______ Sits without help

______ Stands without help

______ Lifts head when lying on stomach

______ Sits with support

Skill to encourage: ______________________________

Way to encourage: ______________________________

______________________________

______ Puts objects in containers

______ Swipes at objects

______ Grabs objects

______ Transfers objects from one hand to the other

Skill to encourage: ______________________________

Way to encourage: ______________________________

______________________________

______ Rolls from stomach to back

______ Creeps on stomach

______ Crawls well

______ Rocks on stomach, waving arms and legs

Skill to encourage: ______________________________

Way to encourage: ______________________________

______________________________

______ Grasps with thumb and forefinger

______ Shakes rattle

______ Bangs blocks together

______ Puts objects to mouth

Skill to encourage: ______________________________

Way to encourage: ______________________________

______________________________

Name ______________________ Date ______________ Class ______________

# Study Guide

CHAPTER 14

Caring for Infants

**Directions:** Complete the items that follow in the space provided.

1. What are four reasons a baby might cry?

2. Suggest six ways to soothe a baby.

3. In each situation below, explain what the baby is signaling and how the parent can respond.

   The baby's eyes widen as they focus on a toy the parent is holding. The baby stops moving his arms and legs as he tracks the movement of the toy.

   After watching her mother's face for several minutes as the mother talks and sings to the baby, the infant turns her head away and draws up her legs.

4. Why do newborns need to be fed so frequently?

5. Is breast-feeding uncomfortable for a mother? Explain.

6. Why should baby bottles NOT be heated in a microwave?

7. Explain how to burp a baby.

8. Give five recommendations for introducing a child to solid food.

9. What are some examples of good foods for a baby learning to self-feed?

(Continued on next page)

10. What should you have within easy reach when changing a baby's diaper?

11. What is a general rule for how many layers of clothing a baby needs?

12. Explain when you would give a baby a sponge bath, a bath in a baby tub, and a bath in the regular bathtub.

13. Name four actions that can help lower the risk of SIDS.

14. What do well-baby examinations include?

15. What does immunizing a baby do?

16. When should parents call the doctor for advice about a sick child?

17. When should parents call 911?

18. How do infant games, like patty-cake, help promote a baby's development?

19. Offer three ways for parents to promote a baby's emotional and social development.

Name ______________________ Date ______________ Class ______________



# A Day in the Life of a Baby

**Part I. Directions:** Select an age from birth to one year. Write down what you would consider a typical daily schedule for an infant of this age. Include feedings, diaper changes, bathing, being held, awake time with an adult nearby, and sleeping. Answers will vary.

Early morning: ______________________

Mid-morning: ______________________

Late morning: ______________________

Early afternoon: ______________________

Mid-afternoon: ______________________

Late afternoon: ______________________

Early evening: ______________________

Late evening: ______________________

During the night: ______________________

**Part II. Directions:** Interview the parent of an infant who is under a year old. Ask the parent what a "typical" day for the baby is and write the answers in the time slots below.

Early morning: ______________________

Mid-morning: ______________________

Late morning: ______________________

Early afternoon: ______________________

(Continued on next page)

A Day in the Life of a Baby (continued)

Mid-afternoon: ______________________________________________

______________________________________________

Late afternoon: ______________________________________________

______________________________________________

Early evening: ______________________________________________

______________________________________________

Late evening: ______________________________________________

______________________________________________

During the night: ______________________________________________

______________________________________________

How does this actual schedule compare with the one you came up with? Did any findings surprise you? Why or why not?

______________________________________________

______________________________________________

______________________________________________

______________________________________________

______________________________________________

______________________________________________

______________________________________________

______________________________________________

______________________________________________

______________________________________________

______________________________________________

______________________________________________

______________________________________________

______________________________________________

______________________________________________

______________________________________________

Name ______________________ Date ______________ Class ______________

CHAPTER 14

Caring for Infants

# Off to the Grocery Store

**Part I. Directions:** Go to the baby food aisle of a grocery store, or research baby food products on the Internet or in print resources, to answer the following questions.

### Infant Formula

1. What types are available? ______________________
2. Read the packages and calculate cost per serving. Compare powdered and ready-to-use formula.
   Cost per serving: ______________________
   Preparation required: ______________________
   Other differences: ______________________
3. What supplements do the formulas contain? What is their purpose or value?
   ______________________
4. Why do some formulas contain no milk base? ______________________

### Baby Cereals

5. What types are available? ______________________
6. Is more than one style or brand available? Explain. ______________________
   ______________________
7. What differences do you find among types, styles, or brands, such as price and ingredients?
   ______________________

### Baby Food in Jars

8. Why are the jars marked 1, 2, and 3? ______________________
   ______________________
9. What types of foods are in each group?
   Jars marked 1: ______________________
   Jars marked 2: ______________________
   Jars marked 3: ______________________
10. What differences do you find among types, styles, or brands, such as price and ingredients?
    ______________________
    ______________________

### Finger Foods

11. What finger foods are available for older infants?
    ______________________
12. What differences do you find among types, styles, or brands, such as price and ingredients?
    ______________________

(Continued on next page)

Off to the Grocery Store (continued)

**Part II. Directions:** Use your research and other information sources to complete the items that follow.

1. Fill in the table to compare the advantages and disadvantages of formula and breast milk.

| | Powdered Formula | Ready-to-use Formula | Breast Milk |
|---|---|---|---|
| Nutrition | | | |
| Cost | | | |
| Convenience | | | |
| Other advantages | | | |
| Other disadvantages | | | |

2. What factors might influence parents when choosing between breast milk, powdered formula, and ready-to-use formula?

3. Fill in the table to compare the advantages and disadvantages of different forms of baby food.

| | Baby Cereals | Baby Food in Jars | Homemade Baby Foods |
|---|---|---|---|
| Nutrition | | | |
| Cost | | | |
| Convenience | | | |
| Other advantages | | | |
| Other disadvantages | | | |

4. Using the information gathered for item 3 above, draw conclusions about which type of baby food you would choose to feed your infant. Be sure to give reasons to support your conclusions.

Name ______________________ Date ______________ Class ______________

# Study Guide

CHAPTER **15**

**Meeting Children's Physical Needs**

**Directions:** Complete the items that follow in the space provided.

1. Why is it helpful for parents to know what to expect at different stages of a child's development?

2. Summarize the physical growth children and teens experience during each of the following periods.

   Toddler years: ______________________

   Preschool years: ______________________

   School-age years: ______________________

   Adolescence: ______________________

3. What is manual dexterity?

4. When do children begin to lose their primary teeth? When are all the permanent teeth usually in? What are wisdom teeth?

5. Complete the nutrient chart below.

| Nutrients | What They Do | Examples of Foods |
|---|---|---|
| Protein | | |
| Carbohydrates | | |
| Vitamins and minerals | | |
| Fats | | |
| Water | | |

(Continued on next page)

6. What is a calorie? What factors determine calorie needs?

7. What factors should parents remember about serving food to children at meals?

8. Give two examples of nutritious snacks for children.

9. How can parents promote good eating habits in children?

10. How might parents deal with a child who is a finicky eater?

11. List two ways to make learning to self-feed easier for a toddler.

12. List four ways parents can prevent and treat obesity in their children.

13. What are the benefits of exercise for children?

14. How can parents promote physical activity for children?

15. Define large motor skills and small motor skills.

16. What are three large motor development milestones from ages one to five?

(Continued on next page)

17. What are three ways to encourage children's development in small motor skills?

_______________

_______________

_______________

18. What does ambidextrous mean?

_______________

19. In addition to being clean, how do good personal hygiene skills benefit children?

_______________

20. How can parents promote good hygiene habits in children?

_______________

_______________

21. How can parents make bathing a pleasant and fun experience for small children?

_______________

22. What are sphincter muscles?

_______________

23. What are four signs that a child is ready to be toilet trained?

_______________

_______________

_______________

_______________

24. What is enuresis?

_______________

25. How can parents help children develop good sleeping habits?

_______________

_______________

26. What are two guidelines for establishing bedtime routines?

_______________

_______________

27. Name three safety guidelines for children's clothing.

_______________

_______________

_______________

28. What other factors affect clothing choices?

_______________

_______________

Name ______________________ Date ______________ Class ______________



# Family Fun

**Directions:** Many activities that are fun for the whole family can help children develop motor skills. For each age group below, suggest a family activity that can help develop large motor skills and one that can help develop small motor skills. Be sure to list a different activity each time. Also identify at least one specific skill each activity can develop. An example has been completed for you.

| | Large Motor Skills | Small Motor Skills |
|---|---|---|
| Toddlers | Family Activity:<br>Rolling ball to each other on lawn<br><br>Skill(s) Promoted:<br>Running (chasing ball), scooping up ball in arms | Family Activity:<br><br>Skill(s) Promoted: |
| Preschoolers | Family Activity:<br><br>Skill(s) Promoted: | Family Activity:<br><br>Skill(s) Promoted: |
| School-Age Children | Family Activity:<br><br>Skill(s) Promoted: | Family Activity:<br><br>Skill(s) Promoted: |
| Adolescents | Family Activity:<br><br>Skill(s) Promoted: | Family Activity:<br><br>Skill(s) Promoted: |

Name ______________________ Date ____________ Class ____________



# What Should a Three-Year-Old Eat?

**Directions:** In the chart below, plan a day's menu for an active three-year-old. List the foods to serve and the amounts. Be sure the amounts for each food group add up to the recommended daily total. When you have completed your menu, answer the questions on the next page.

| | **Grain Group** | **Vegetable Group** | **Fruit Group** | **Milk Group** | **Meat & Beans Group** |
|---|---|---|---|---|---|
| **Recommended amounts** | 5 ounces | 1½ cups | 1½ cups | 2 cups | 4 ounces |
| **Breakfast** | | | | | |
| **Snack** | | | | | |
| **Lunch** | | | | | |
| **Snack** | | | | | |
| **Dinner** | | | | | |
| **Snack** | | | | | |
| **Total amounts** | | | | | |

(Continued on next page)

1. Does your menu include the recommended amount of each food group for a child of this age? If not, what improvements could you make?

2. Are any foods high in fat, sugar, or salt? If so, which ones?

3. What different shapes of food are represented in the menu? How could variety of shape be improved?

4. Does each meal include a variety of colors? If so, explain why. If not, what improvements could you make?

5. Does each meal include a variety of food textures? If so, explain why. If not, what improvements could you make?

Name ____________________ Date ____________ Class ____________

# Study Guide

CHAPTER 16

Health and Safety

**Directions:** Complete the items that follow in the space provided.

1. What strategies are included in a wellness approach to life?

2. What does preventive health care for children include?

3. What is developmental screening? Why is it important?

4. How might parents know if their small child is not feeling well?

5. Name some common childhood illnesses that can often be treated at home.

6. What general guidelines should parents or caregivers follow in caring for ill children?

7. Describe how parents should treat the following common childhood illnesses.

   A cold: ____________________

   Diarrhea: ____________________

   Influenza: ____________________

8. What does chronic illness mean? Name three chronic illnesses that children might have.

(Continued on next page)

9. How can parents make a child feel more comfortable if the child needs to go to the hospital?

10. Name at least six ways to make a home safe for young children.

11. What steps can parents take to make sure their children's toys are safe for them?

12. How might children get lead poisoning in the home? What actions can parents take to prevent this?

13. How can parents keep children safe on the playground?

14. Name four ways parents can prevent children from drowning.

15. What safety measures does a driver need to take to prevent injuries to children?

(Continued on next page)

16. What should parents and caregivers teach children about pedestrian and bicycle safety?

17. Give four guidelines that can help parents protect their children from strangers who might harm them.

18. Describe treatment for two common injuries in children.

19. What is shock?

20. What is first aid?

21. What is CPR? Who should administer CPR?

22. Name some general guidelines for handling a serious injury to a child.

23. Name five types of information parents should give a temporary caregiver.

Name ______________________ Date __________ Class __________



# Good Idea or Bad Idea?

**Directions:** Read each situation below. If you think the adult's behavior is the correct thing to do, write "Good idea" in the space provided. If you think the behavior is incorrect, write "Bad idea" and explain what the adult should do instead.

1. Yvonne keeps emergency phone numbers programmed into her phone. She had her older children practice dialing the emergency numbers and giving the correct information when they reached help.

______________________

______________________

______________________

2. Angelica's five-year-old burned her hand. Angelica washed the burned area and applied a cream.

______________________

______________________

______________________

3. Joshua's five-year-old had a nosebleed, so he had the child tip his head back to stop the bleeding.

______________________

______________________

______________________

4. Nico fell off his bike and broke his arm. His dad put a folded jacket under Nico's arm and called for medical help on his cell phone.

______________________

______________________

______________________

5. Craig's six-year-old was running a fever. Craig needed to go to work, so he sent his son to school.

______________________

______________________

______________________

6. Brittany took her two small children to the beach. While they were wading in the water, she decided to lie back, close her eyes, and rest for a while.

______________________

______________________

______________________

Name ______________________________ Date ________________ Class ________



# First Aid

**Directions:** For each medical situation described below, consider what steps a parent or caregiver should take and in what order. Evaluate the possible actions listed under each situation.

- Write "0" beside each step the parent or caregiver should NOT take in that situation.
- Write a "1" beside the first step the caregiver should take, a "2" beside the second step, and so forth.

1. A child burns his or her finger on the stove. What steps should the caregiver take?

   ______ Wrap a bandage over the area of the burn.
   ______ Rub the finger vigorously with a clean towel.
   ______ Run cold water over the finger for five minutes.
   ______ Give the child an aspirin to relieve the pain.
   ______ Keep the area around the burn clean and dry.
   ______ Apply ointment to the area of the burn.

2. A child falls and breaks his or her arm. What steps should the caregiver take?

   ______ Keep the child still.
   ______ Have the child walk until help arrives.
   ______ Place a pillow under the injured arm.
   ______ Move the arm back and forth to keep it flexible.
   ______ Try to rotate the arm back into its proper position.
   ______ Call the child's health care provider.

3. A child gets a splinter in his or her hand. What steps should the caregiver take?

   ______ Clean the area of the splinter with antiseptic.
   ______ Remove the splinter with a sterilized needle or tweezers.
   ______ Sterilize the exposed part of the splinter with a match.
   ______ Cut off the exposed part of the splinter with scissors.
   ______ Phone emergency services for an ambulance.
   ______ Wash the area around the splinter.

(Continued on next page)

4. A child, coughing hard, tells the caregiver that he or she is choking on a piece of food. What steps should the caregiver take?

_____ Have the child lie face up on the floor.

_____ Give the child additional food as a "chaser."

_____ Lay the child's stomach across the caregiver's lap.

_____ Give the child five sharp blows to the back with the heel of the hand.

_____ Wait for the choking to clear on its own so long as the child can cough.

_____ Give the child mouth-to-mouth resuscitation.

5. A child cuts his or her hand on a piece of broken glass. What steps should the caregiver take?

_____ Place a bandage over the cut.

_____ Dry the area of the cut.

_____ Remove any scraped skin from around the cut.

_____ Apply pressure to stop the bleeding, if needed.

_____ Wash the cut with soap and water.

_____ Apply antiseptic to the cut.

6. A child has a high fever with convulsions. What steps should the caregiver take?

_____ Guide the child to a clear space on the floor.

_____ Put a cushion or folded towel under the child's head.

_____ Phone the child's health care provider.

_____ Put the child to sleep on his or her back.

_____ Turn the child to one side to let saliva drain from the mouth.

_____ Wait for convulsions to stop.

7. A child's foot is stung by a bee. The child's painful reaction is localized in the foot; the rest of the body seems unaffected. What steps should the caregiver take?

_____ Pull out the stinger with sterilized tweezers.

_____ Disinfect the site of the sting.

_____ Apply heat to the foot to reduce the swelling.

_____ Scrape or brush off the stinger with a credit card or similar object.

_____ Apply ice or cold packs to the child's foot.

_____ Use your fingers to withdraw the stinger from the foot.

Name ______________________ Date ______________ Class ______________

# Study Guide

CHAPTER **17**

**Helping Children Learn**

**Directions:** Complete the items that follow in the space provided.

1. Summarize the development of the brain from birth through adolescence.

2. List the names of Piaget's stages of intellectual development, the age covered by each stage, and the characteristics that describe children's thinking in each stage.

| Stage | Ages | Characteristics |
|---|---|---|
| | | |
| | | |
| | | |
| | | |

3. Define the following principles that children learn, according to Piaget.

Conservation: ______________________

Concepts: ______________________

Seriation: ______________________

Classification: ______________________

Reversibility: ______________________

(Continued on next page)

4. How does Howard Gardner's theory of intelligence differ from Jean Piaget's?

5. How do parents act as teachers to their children?

6. Describe ways parents can help children develop skills in the following areas.
   Basic concepts such as classification, shape, size and space, number and quantity, and time:

   Thinking:

   Vocabulary:

   Reading and writing:

   Math:

7. Explain the value of art and music experiences for children.

Name ______________________ Date ______________ Class ______________



# Check It Out

**Directions:** Go to the children's section of a community library or a local bookstore, or telephone one. Talk with the librarian or clerk about how to determine suitable books for children of different ages. For each age level below, find at least one book at the library, store, or on the Internet. Write down the title, author, a two- or three-sentence summary of the book, and what makes it appropriate for that age level.

**Two-year-olds**

Title: ______________________________

Author: ______________________________

Summary: ______________________________

______________________________

Age-appropriate features: ______________________________

**Four-year-olds**

Title: ______________________________

Author: ______________________________

Summary: ______________________________

______________________________

Age-appropriate features: ______________________________

**Six-year-olds**

Title: ______________________________

Author: ______________________________

Summary: ______________________________

______________________________

Age-appropriate features: ______________________________

**Ten-year-olds**

Title: ______________________________

Author: ______________________________

Summary: ______________________________

______________________________

Age-appropriate features: ______________________________

Name ______________________ Date ______________ Class ______________



# Everyday Learning

**Directions:** In the space provided, explain how a parent might use the following everyday situations as learning opportunities for a child. Use your text and Internet or print references as resources for your answers.

1. Taking a three-year-old for a walk in the park.

______________________________________________

______________________________________________

______________________________________________

2. Taking a seven-year-old to the library.

______________________________________________

______________________________________________

______________________________________________

3. Folding laundry with a four-year-old.

______________________________________________

______________________________________________

______________________________________________

4. Making cookies with a six-year-old.

______________________________________________

______________________________________________

______________________________________________

5. Shopping for groceries with an eight-year-old.

______________________________________________

______________________________________________

______________________________________________

6. Going to the post office with a five-year-old.

______________________________________________

______________________________________________

______________________________________________

7. Helping a two-year-old get dressed.

______________________________________________

______________________________________________

______________________________________________

Name ______________________ Date ______________ Class ______________



# TV or Not TV?

**Part I. Directions:** Fill in the chart to show factors that would influence how you, as a parent, might decide your television-watching policy for each of the three age groups shown on the chart.

| | Birth to 2 years | 3 to 5 years | 7 to 10 years |
|---|---|---|---|
| Advantages of TV | | | |
| Disadvantages of TV | | | |
| Type of programming, if any | | | |
| Other considerations | | | |

**Part II. Directions:** Based on the information in the chart, define and explain your television watching policy for each of the three age groups.

**Birth to 2 years**

Policy: ______________________

Reason: ______________________

**3 to 5 years**

Policy: ______________________

Reason: ______________________

**7 to 10 years**

Policy: ______________________

Reason: ______________________

Name ______________________ Date ______________ Class ______________

CHAPTER 17

Helping Children Learn

# The Arts in a Child's Life

**Directions:** Fill in the items below to suggest activities for each age group in music, art, and drama or dance. Also explain how these activities can help children learn, referring to skills, qualities, or concepts such as these or others:

- Classification, shape, size, space, number, quantity, or time
- Memory and reasoning
- Curiosity, imagination, and creativity
- Language

**Music**

1. Two activities for toddlers and preschoolers: ______________________
2. Two activities for school-age children: ______________________
3. Two activities for adolescents: ______________________
4. Three ways music can help children learn (explain each):

______________________

______________________

______________________

**Art**

5. Two activities for toddlers and preschoolers: ______________________
6. Two activities for school-age children: ______________________
7. Two activities for adolescents: ______________________
8. Three ways art can help children learn (explain each):

______________________

______________________

______________________

**Drama or dance**

9. One activity for toddlers and preschoolers: ______________________
10. One activity for school-age children: ______________________
11. One activity for adolescents: ______________________
12. One way drama or dance can help children learn (explain):

______________________

Name ______________________ Date ____________ Class ____________

# Study Guide

CHAPTER 18

Meeting Children's Emotional Needs

**Directions:** Complete the items that follow in the space provided.

1. What is temperament? ______________________
2. Describe emotional development from infancy through adolescence.

______________________

3. The theory of personality developed by psychologist Sigmund Freud defines three aspects of thought and feeling, or levels of awareness about emotions. Explain what each involves and at what age it develops.

   Id: ______________________

   Ego: ______________________

   Superego: ______________________

4. Explain Erikson's theory of social and emotional development.

______________________

5. How can parents encourage children's need for independence?

______________________

(Continued on next page)

6. How do children with a positive self-image view themselves? How do children with a negative self-image view themselves?

7. What is the difference between self-confidence and self-centeredness? What can happen if children think too highly of themselves?

8. Name four things parents can do to help their children develop self-esteem.

9. Why is it important for parents to show affection toward their children?

10. What is empathy? How does having empathy help a child relate to others?

11. Name four ways parents can teach compassion to their children.

12. How can parents help their children deal with feelings of jealousy?

(Continued on next page)

13. Name three ways sensitive parents can help children cope with fears.

14. What are three things parents can do to help children with separation anxiety?

15. What strategies can parents use to deal with anger in children?

16. What is negativism? At what age do children display this behavior? Why do they act this way?

17. List three ways parents can deal with children's negativism.

18. Identify two major sources of stress for children and two everyday causes of stress.

19. How can parents help their adolescent children manage stress?

20. What is anxiety? How can parents help their children when they feel anxious?

(Continued on next page)

21. How is an anxiety disorder different from anxiety? What symptoms may indicate an anxiety disorder?

22. Describe the difference between anorexia nervosa and bulimia nervosa.

23. What are three symptoms of an eating disorder? If parents notice these symptoms, what should they do?

24. How can parents reduce the risk of eating disorders in their children?

25. Everyone feels "down" once in a while. What distinguishes depression from just feeling down?

26. List six guidelines for parents concerning suicide.

27. Where can parents go for help if their child is showing signs of serious emotional problems?

Name ______________________ Date ______________ Class ______________



# Feelings

**Directions:** Feelings are neither right nor wrong. Children—and adults—may feel happy, sad, loving, angry, anxious, jealous, or calm in various situations. While children cannot *control* how they feel, they can learn how to *express* their feelings in appropriate ways. For each of the following situations, suggest how a parent might respond to help the child learn to express his or her feelings appropriately.

1. The family dog has died and ten-year-old Marlon is in his room, crying. If you were Marlon's parent, what would you say to help comfort him? Suggest at least three things to say to him.

2. Eight-year-old Tamika is getting dressed for her softball game. In previous games she played an outfield position, but today she is scheduled to pitch. She is so anxious that she is near tears. If you were Tamika's parent, how would you help calm her nervousness? Suggest at least three things to say to her.

3. Nine-year-old Lorenzo was excited that he received the highest grade in the class on a particular assignment. He boasted to his friends on the way home from school. They turned away from him and didn't invite him to join in their after-school plans. Now Lorenzo is upset and angry with his friends. If you were Lorenzo's parent, what advice would you give him?

4. Robby was playing tennis with his friends. He became frustrated after missing several shots and threw his racquet down, bending the frame. If you were Robby's parent, what would you say to him?

Name ______________________ Date ____________ Class ____________



# Reducing the "Nos"

**Directions:** Parents can help prevent temper tantrums in a toddler by reducing the number of times the child hears "no" every day. Listed below are some things a toddler might hear from a parent. In the space provided, suggest how the parent could respond differently or change the situation to bring about the desired result without sending a negative message.

1. "Don't touch the glass candy dish on the coffee table."

2. (At the grocery store) "No, I am not buying you candy."

3. "Don't bang your fork on the table."

4. "No, it's too warm to wear your favorite sweater today."

5. "Stop playing with that toy! The noise is driving me crazy!"

6. "Don't touch those pillows. I just straightened them."

7. "Stop pouting."

8. "No, we're not going to the park today because it's raining."

Name ______________________ Date ______________ Class ______________

# Study Guide

CHAPTER **19**

**Helping Children Relate to Others**

**Directions:** Complete the items that follow in the space provided.

1. What is socialization?

2. How might children be affected if they do not learn appropriate social behaviors?

3. Name three ways for parents to strengthen relationships in the family.

4. What type of interaction characterizes toddlers' social play?

5. Describe cooperative play. At what age do children begin cooperative play?

6. Describe the peer relationships of school-age children.

7. Describe peer relationships during adolescence.

8. How can parents help their children respond to bullying?

(Continued on next page)

9. How should parents of a bully respond to their child's actions?

10. What are four things parents can do to help children deal with negative peer pressure?

11. How can parents help a child who has been rejected by peers?

12. What are some ways children learn to interact with adults outside their family?

13. Describe ways for parents to help children learn the following social skills.

Using good manners:

Resolving conflicts:

Overcoming shyness:

14. How can parents help children appreciate diversity?

Name ______________________ Date ______________ Class ______________



# Interacting All Day Long

**Directions:** Imagine a ten-year-old child on an ordinary school day. For each part of the day listed below, briefly describe an interaction the child might experience with another child or adult. Then suggest a good way for the child to handle that interaction. Finally, describe how a parent might help the child learn to handle such a situation. The first one is filled in as an example.

1. Morning, at home with family before school

   Interaction: Hears siblings complain they both want first turn in the bathroom

   Child's response: Distracts one by helping her pack her backpack until other is done

   Parental guidance: Often models ways to act as a peacemaker, praises child for peacemaking

2. In the school yard before school or at recess or lunch break

   Interaction: ______________________

   Child's response: ______________________

   ______________________

   Parental guidance: ______________________

   ______________________

3. In the classroom during school

   Interaction: ______________________

   Child's response: ______________________

   ______________________

   Parental guidance: ______________________

   ______________________

4. Afternoon, in an after-school activity away from home

   Interaction: ______________________

   Child's response: ______________________

   ______________________

   Parental guidance: ______________________

   ______________________

5. At home for dinner or in the evening

   Interaction: ______________________

   Child's response: ______________________

   ______________________

   Parental guidance: ______________________

   ______________________

Name ______________________ Date ______________ Class ______________

CHAPTER 19

Helping Children Relate to Others

# Parents and Teasing

**Directions:** Apply practical reasoning to respond to the items below, based on your thoughts and experiences and what you have learned in Chapter 19.

1. Imagine you are the parent of a child who tells you he or she is unhappy about being teased.

   As the child's parent, what result do you want to achieve in this situation?

   ______________________________________________

   ______________________________________________

   What action might you take to achieve that result?

   ______________________________________________

   ______________________________________________

   What consequences might result from your action, including possible risks?

   ______________________________________________

   ______________________________________________

   How might you respond to possible negative consequences?

   ______________________________________________

   ______________________________________________

2. Imagine you are the parent of a child who is making another child unhappy by teasing him or her.

   As the child's parent, what result do you want to achieve in this situation?

   ______________________________________________

   ______________________________________________

   What action might you take to achieve that result?

   ______________________________________________

   ______________________________________________

   What consequences might result from your action, including possible risks?

   ______________________________________________

   ______________________________________________

   How might you respond to possible negative consequences?

   ______________________________________________

   ______________________________________________

Name ______________________ Date ____________ Class ____________

# Study Guide

CHAPTER 20

The Value of Play

**Directions:** Complete the items that follow in the space provided.

1. What is repetitive play? What do infants learn from this type of play?

2. What type of play do toddlers generally engage in? What does it involve? Give an example.

3. Explain symbolic play. At what ages do children usually engage in symbolic play?

4. Around age five, children become interested in what type of play? How long does this stage of play last?

5. What is exploratory play? Give an example.

6. What physical benefits does play have for children?

7. How do children benefit intellectually from play?

8. Name two benefits a child may gain from playing with a doll or stuffed animal.

9. Name at least three social skills children can learn through group play.

(Continued on next page)

10. How do children develop moral values through play?

11. Describe four general roles parents can take in promoting children's play activities.

12. Name three ways for parents to spend less money on toys.

13. Give one example each of an appropriate toy for infants, toddlers, preschoolers, and school-age children.

14. How can computer and electronic games help a child's development? How might these games be harmful to a child?

15. Describe ways for parents to guide children's activities in the following types of play.

Active play:

Quiet play:

Dramatic play:

Art activities:

Music activities:

16. Why is it important for parents to make play a priority in the family?

Name ______________________ Date ______________ Class ______________



# Let's Play!

**Directions:** For each kind of play and age of child listed below, suggest a play activity a parent might facilitate. Identify two ways the play activity would benefit the child. Circle **P**, **I**, **E**, **S**, or **M** to indicate whether the benefit is physical, intellectual, emotional, social, or moral. (You may circle more than one if appropriate.) Finally, suggest two things the parent could do to facilitate the play activity.

**Repetitive play with a child who is 9 months old**

Suggested play activity: ______________________

Physical, intellectual, emotional, social, or moral benefits for the child:

1. ______________________ (P I E S M)
2. ______________________ (P I E S M)

Ways a parent could facilitate the activity:

1. ______________________
2. ______________________

**Constructive play with a child who is 2 years old**

Suggested play activity: ______________________

Physical, intellectual, emotional, social, or moral benefits for the child:

1. ______________________ (P I E S M)
2. ______________________ (P I E S M)

Ways a parent could facilitate the activity:

1. ______________________
2. ______________________

**Exploratory play with a child who is 3 years old**

Suggested play activity: ______________________

Physical, intellectual, emotional, social, or moral benefits for the child:

1. ______________________ (P I E S M)
2. ______________________ (P I E S M)

Ways a parent could facilitate the activity:

1. ______________________
2. ______________________

(Continued on next page)

**Symbolic play with a child who is 5 years old**

Suggested play activity: ______________________________

Physical, intellectual, emotional, social, or moral benefits for the child:

1. ______________________________ (P I E S M)
2. ______________________________ (P I E S M)

Ways a parent could facilitate the activity:

1. ______________________________
2. ______________________________

**Dramatic play with a child who is 6 years old**

Suggested play activity: ______________________________

Physical, intellectual, emotional, social, or moral benefits for the child:

1. ______________________________ (P I E S M)
2. ______________________________ (P I E S M)

Ways a parent could facilitate the activity:

1. ______________________________
2. ______________________________

**Game play with a child who is 8 years old**

Suggested play activity: ______________________________

Physical, intellectual, emotional, social, or moral benefits for the child:

1. ______________________________ (P I E S M)
2. ______________________________ (P I E S M)

Ways a parent could facilitate the activity:

1. ______________________________
2. ______________________________

**Active play with a child who is 10 years old**

Suggested play activity: ______________________________

Physical, intellectual, emotional, social, or moral benefits for the child:

1. ______________________________ (P I E S M)
2. ______________________________ (P I E S M)

Ways a parent could facilitate the activity:

1. ______________________________
2. ______________________________

Name ______________________ Date ____________ Class ____________

# Study Guide

CHAPTER 21

Communicating with Children

**Directions:** Complete the items that follow in the space provided.

1. Name three benefits of effective communication between parents and children.

2. List four positive ways for parents to use nonverbal communication.

3. What can happen when a parent's verbal and nonverbal messages do not match?

4. Name three guidelines to help parents choose their words with care.

5. Why should parents say "please" and "thank you" to a child?

6. What are the three components of an "I" message?

7. Name three ways to communicate verbally with infants.

8. Besides using a normal tone of voice, what are three guidelines for speaking with toddlers and preschoolers?

9. What are some guidelines for good communication with older children and teens?

(Continued on next page)

10. How can parents really pay attention when their children want to talk to them?

11. Describe how to use active listening when communicating with children.

12. How can parents make time to talk with their children?

13. How do open-ended questions help spark conversation?

14. How can parents promote honesty in children's communication? Give three suggestions.

15. What are social conventions? Give two examples. Why is it important for children to know and use social conventions?

16. What should parents teach children about discussing upsetting topics? Why?

17. Why is it so important for parents to communicate their love and acceptance to children?

Name ______________________ Date ______________ Class ______________



# Choosing Your Words

**Directions:** Listed below are negative statements that a parent might make to a child. Briefly describe the effect each statement might have on the child or the parent-child relationship. Then suggest an alternative wording the parent could use to communicate the same message more positively.

1. "You're always making everyone late! Why can't you ever get ready on time?"

   Effect: ______________________

   Positive wording: ______________________

2. "You're such a lazy child. You make other people do all the work."

   Effect: ______________________

   Positive wording: ______________________

3. "Look how nicely your sister did her homework. You should try harder to be like your sister."

   Effect: ______________________

   Positive wording: ______________________

4. "Stop that! Don't touch that vase! You'll break it!"

   Effect: ______________________

   Positive wording: ______________________

5. "You were a bad child to go outside when I told you to stay in."

   Effect: ______________________

   Positive wording: ______________________

6. "Shut up! I can't stand that horrible noise!"

   Effect: ______________________

   Positive wording: ______________________

Name ______________________ Date ______________ Class ______________

CHAPTER 21

Communicating with Children

# Making Communication Age-Appropriate

**Directions:** Parents need to word their communications to fit the age of the child. Four children of different ages are listed below. For each statement that follows, choose the child for whom the statement is most age-appropriate and explain your reasoning.

**Children**
Andrew, age 8 months
Betsy, age 4 years
Carl, age 8 years
Darcy, age 14 years

1. "Before we go out in the cold, put on your sweater and knit cap and bring along a jacket."
   Child: ______________ Reason: ______________________________

2. "We'd better wrap you up warm, warm, warm. Feel the fuzzy-wuzzy sweater. Feel how fuzzy and warm. First one arm and then the other. You'll be warm, warm, warm out in the cold, cold, cold."
   Child: ______________ Reason: ______________________________

3. "Put on something warm. It's cold out there, and you don't want to get sick before your big game on Saturday."
   Child: ______________ Reason: ______________________________

4. "Get your sweater." (pause) "Good. Now get your knit cap."
   Child: ______________ Reason: ______________________________

5. "It feels like we're heading into a second Ice Age. Better put on a sweater!"
   Child: ______________ Reason: ______________________________

Name ______________________ Date ______________ Class ______________

## Study Guide

CHAPTER 22

Building Children's Character

**Directions:** Complete the items that follow in the space provided.

1. How does character affect individuals? In what ways does it ultimately affect society?

2. Explain Kohlberg's first level of moral development.

3. What level of moral development begins around the ages of 9 to 15? Describe.

4. How do people who have reached Kohlberg's highest level of moral development behave?

5. Discuss the five ways Bronfenbrenner believed people think about right and wrong.

6. Explain what is meant by a conscience. At what age do children develop a conscience?

(Continued on next page)

7. List four strategies for teaching values to children.

8. What are six values parents should teach their children?

9. How do children develop a strong work ethic?

10. Explain what parents might do when their children think a situation is unfair.

11. How can parents help their children make wise ethical choices?

12. How do peers influence children's character development?

13. How can parents of an older child respond if their child's friends have very different values from theirs?

14. How might children be influenced by what they see on television?

15. How can parents limit negative influences of television and the Internet? Share two suggestions for each.

Name ______________________ Date ____________ Class ____________

CHAPTER 22

Building Children's Character

# Matching Theories to Practice

**Part I. Directions:** Lawrence Kohlberg's six stages of moral development are briefly summarized below. Read each situation that follows and decide which stage it best describes. Write the number of the stage in the blank provided.

**Kohlberg's Stages of Moral Development**

Stage 1. Obedience
Stage 2. Self-interest
Stage 3. Seeking approval
Stage 4. Rules and fairness
Stage 5. Helping others
Stage 6. Universal principles

_______ A. Lydia takes a lost child back home even though it leaves her less time to play.

_______ B. Justin shares a treat with his friend so his friend will share a treat with him.

_______ C. Maria does her homework very neatly so the teacher will notice and praise her.

_______ D. Stephen participates in peaceful civil disobedience for a cause he believes in.

_______ E. Emily puts on her pajamas because her mother told her to.

_______ F. Peter waits his turn in line at the store instead of pushing ahead of others.

**Part II. Directions:** Now make up your own example to illustrate each stage of moral development according to Kohlberg's theory.

1. Obedience: ______________________

2. Self-interest: ______________________

3. Seeking approval: ______________________

4. Rules and fairness: ______________________

5. Helping others: ______________________

6. Universal principles: ______________________

(Continued on next page)

**Part III. Directions:** Urie Bronfennbrenner identified five different moral orientations, or ways in which people might focus their thinking about right and wrong. Read each situation that follows and decide which moral orientation it best describes. Write the name of the moral orientation in the blank provided.

**Bronfenbrenner's Moral Orientations**

- Self-oriented morality
- Authority-oriented morality
- Peer-oriented morality
- Collective-oriented morality
- Objectively-oriented morality

1. A student decides to stop eating junk food because her best friend decided to eat more healthfully.
   Moral orientation: ______________________________
2. A student helps out with the team fundraiser because she feels strong loyalty to the team.
   Moral orientation: ______________________________
3. A student buys the last three hats in the store, even though she knows her friends wanted to buy some too.
   Moral orientation: ______________________________
4. A student takes time to play with a shy child, even though her friends say it's a waste of time.
   Moral orientation: ______________________________
5. A student runs to get to school on time because the teacher told all students to arrive on time.
   Moral orientation: ______________________________

**Part IV. Directions:** Now make up your own example to illustrate each moral orientation according to Bronfenbrenner's theory.

1. Self-oriented morality: ______________________________
   ______________________________
2. Authority-oriented morality: ______________________________
   ______________________________
3. Peer-oriented morality: ______________________________
   ______________________________
4. Collective-oriented morality: ______________________________
   ______________________________
5. Objectively-oriented morality: ______________________________
   ______________________________

Name ______________________ Date ______________ Class ______________

## Study Guide

CHAPTER 23

Promoting Positive Behavior

**Directions:** Complete the items that follow in the space provided.

1. How does discipline differ from punishment?

2. What is meant by positive guidance? What long-term goals can positive guidance help children achieve?

3. Why is it important for parents to show consistency in enforcing rules?

4. What are limits? How do they help children?

5. What might happen to children who are not given limits?

6. What do parents need to understand in order to set specific limits for their children?

7. Describe four principles for setting limits for children.

8. How should parents effectively communicate their expectations to children?

(Continued on next page)

9. What are three techniques for encouraging positive behavior in children?

10. Define positive reinforcement and explain two types.

11. What are six guidelines that will help make positive reinforcement effective?

12. What advantages are there to preventing behavior problems before they begin?

13. How does providing a child-friendly environment help prevent negative behavior?

14. How might a parent ward off potential negative behavior in a child who seems bored?

15. Why do children often respond better when given choices rather than being told what to do? What are two guidelines for parents to follow when giving children choices?

16. Besides providing a child-friendly environment, offering constructive activities, and offering children choices, what can parents do to prevent misbehavior?

17. How does having confidence help parents guide their children effectively?

Name ______________________________ Date ______________ Class ______________



# Planning Positive Guidance

**Part I. Directions:** Twice recently, eight-year-old Justin went to another child's house without telling his parents where he was. Fill in the items to suggest how his parents might plan effective positive guidance.

1. What values will guide Justin's parents in deciding what limits to set?

   ______________________________________________

2. What is an appropriate expectation for Justin's behavior?

   ______________________________________________

3. How might the parents model the behavior?

   ______________________________________________

4. How might the parents teach the behavior?

   ______________________________________________

5. How might the parents coach the behavior?

   ______________________________________________

6. What positive reinforcement can the parents give when Justin behaves appropriately?

   ______________________________________________

   ______________________________________________

**Part II. Directions:** Three-year-old Patricia turns on the television every time she gets a chance and just sits there watching it. Her parents think she spends too much time watching television. Fill in the items to suggest how her parents might plan effective positive guidance.

1. What values will guide Patricia's parents in deciding what limits to set?

   ______________________________________________

2. What is an appropriate expectation for Patricia's behavior?

   ______________________________________________

3. How might the parents model the behavior?

   ______________________________________________

4. How might the parents teach the behavior?

   ______________________________________________

5. How might the parents coach the behavior?

   ______________________________________________

6. What positive reinforcement can the parents give when Patricia behaves appropriately?

   ______________________________________________

   ______________________________________________

Name ______________________ Date ______________ Class ______________

CHAPTER 23

Promoting Positive Behavior

# Evaluating Limits

**Directions:** Fill in the items below to evaluate the limits described and to suggest improvements.

1. A parent says to a 12-year-old, "I know you stayed up until ten o'clock the last few nights, but your bedtime is eight o'clock. Your mother and I want some time alone."

   Is this limit age-appropriate, too loose, or too restrictive? Explain. ______________________

   ______________________________________________

   What is the teaching or guiding purpose of the limit, if any? ______________________

   ______________________________________________

   Is the limit consistent and specific? Explain. ______________________

   ______________________________________________

   What would be more appropriate for the parent to say? ______________________

   ______________________________________________

2. A parent says to a three-year-old, "You need to be careful when you use Mommy's good china. It's very old and valuable and we'd be very sad if it got broken."

   Is this limit age-appropriate, too loose, or too restrictive? Explain. ______________________

   ______________________________________________

   What is the teaching or guiding purpose of the limit, if any? ______________________

   ______________________________________________

   Is the limit consistent and specific? Explain. ______________________

   ______________________________________________

   What would be more appropriate for the parent to say? ______________________

   ______________________________________________

3. A parent says to a 15-year-old, "Have fun going out with your friends Monday night, but get home by a reasonable hour. Remember, we always ask you to do that on school nights."

   Is this limit age-appropriate, too loose, or too restrictive? Explain. ______________________

   ______________________________________________

   What is the teaching or guiding purpose of the limit, if any? ______________________

   ______________________________________________

   Is the limit consistent and specific? Explain. ______________________

   ______________________________________________

   What would be more appropriate for the parent to say? ______________________

   ______________________________________________

Name ______________________ Date ______________ Class ______________

# Study Guide

CHAPTER 24

Handling Negative Behavior

**Directions:** Complete the items that follow in the space provided.

1. Name six reasons children might misbehave.

2. How is knowing the reason a child is misbehaving helpful to parents?

3. How can parents show understanding of a child's emotions yet respond appropriately to inappropriate expressions of those emotions?

4. When analyzing a child's negative behavior, what are six things for parents to consider?

5. For what reason might a parent ignore a child's negative behavior?

6. What are three situations in which redirecting a child's misbehavior might be appropriate?

7. What might be a parent's first choice of response when a child breaks a rule he or she is still learning?

8. What is the difference between natural consequences and logical consequences? Give an example of each.

(Continued on next page)

9. For logical consequences to be effective, what four guidelines should parents follow?

10. What are the advantages of time-out?

11. Name four inappropriate responses to children's negative behavior. Discuss why each is inappropriate.

12. How can parents respond when they believe a child is using inappropriate language to get a reaction from them?

13. Name three ways parents can handle their children's aggression.

14. How can parents make it easier for their children to tell the truth?

15. Offer four ways for parents to respond to a child's theft.

16. What help is available for children who exhibit a serious behavior problem?

Name _______________ Date _______________ Class _______________



# Consequences

**Directions:** For each situation described below, suggest and evaluate an appropriate consequence.

1. During her evening bath, five-year-old Danielle splashes bath water all over the bathroom, even though she has been told consistently that the bath water is supposed to stay in the bathtub.

   Appropriate consequence: _______________

   Is this a natural or logical consequence? How is it related to the behavior? _______________

   How is it important to the child? _______________

   How is it proportional to the behavior? _______________

   How is it timely? _______________

2. Although ten-year-old Jason knows that rough play is only for outdoors, he and his friends roughhouse in the house and the television screen gets broken.

   Appropriate consequence: _______________

   Is this a natural or logical consequence? How is it related to the behavior? _______________

   How is it important to the child? _______________

   How is it proportional to the behavior? _______________

   How is it timely? _______________

3. On a Saturday night, 15-year-old Lucy stays out half an hour past curfew.

   Appropriate consequence: _______________

   Is this a natural or logical consequence? How is it related to the behavior? _______________

   How is it important to the child? _______________

   How is it proportional to the behavior? _______________

   How is it timely? _______________

Name ______________________ Date ____________ Class ____________



# Positive Responses to Negative Behavior

**Directions:** When young children's behavior is not acceptable, parents' first reaction often is to say "no" to them. However, parents who find another way to handle the situation not only stop negative behavior but turn the situation into a learning experience. Read each of the following situations and suggest how the parent might respond.

1. Two-year-old Graham bangs his toy hammer on the television screen.

2. Three-year-old Shakira goes into the new baby's room and tries to wake him.

3. Aidan and Renee's friends come for a visit and bring their toddler. As the child plays with Aidan and Renee's toddler, one grabs a toy from the other. The other child starts to cry.

4. Three-year-old Taylor picks up a fragile figurine from the coffee table.

5. Michael is five. He is playing in the backyard with several friends. Michael wants to be first in all the games and play with the toys he likes the best.

6. In the grocery store, two-year-old Luisa begins to have a tantrum when her mother says that she is going to buy crackers instead of the cookies Luisa likes.

Name ______________________ Date ______________ Class ______________

# Study Guide



**Directions:** Complete the items that follow in the space provided.

1. What are three general conditions that may cause special needs?

2. Define *disability*.

3. List six general categories of disabilities.

4. Name at least three characteristics of children with cognitive impairments.

5. What are two types of sensory impairments?

6. What parts of the body are affected by orthopedic impairments? What treatment might children affected by these impairments receive?

7. What types of problems might children with learning disorders have?

8. What are four behaviors that might indicate a child has an emotional or behavioral disorder?

9. Explain ADHD.

(Continued on next page)

10. Compare autism with Asperger's syndrome.

11. Describe the impact on family members of a child with a disability.

12. How should parents treat their child with a disability?

13. How can parents advocate for their child with a disability?

14. What are four types of educational resources children with disabilities can take advantage of?

15. Name five types of private and community resources for children and families.

16. How can parents help children who are gifted and talented with their social skills? Their educational needs?

# The Road to Acceptance

**Directions:** Learning that one's child has a disability is never easy. Nancy and Paul have taken their second child, 18-month-old Jeffrey, to the doctor to ask why Jeffrey hasn't started speaking. The doctor has just told them that Jeffrey has severe hearing loss that is probably irreversible. Fill in the items below to follow Nancy and Paul on the road to acceptance.

1. What are three questions Nancy and Paul might ask the doctor?

2. Describe four emotions Nancy and Paul might experience in the weeks that follow.

3. What might Nancy and Paul tell their parents and other relatives about Jeffrey's hearing loss?

4. What might Nancy and Paul tell their six-year-old daughter about Jeffrey's hearing loss?

5. How might Jeffrey's disability affect how Paul and Nancy interact with their six-year-old?

6. What are three ways Nancy and Paul can nurture their relationship while caring for a child with special needs?

(Continued on next page)

7. Describe some ways Nancy and Paul will treat Jeffrey the same as they would treat a hearing child.

8. Describe some ways Nancy and Paul will treat Jeffrey differently because of his hearing loss.

9. What are two ways Nancy and Paul can find out about community and government resources?

10. As Jeffrey gets older, what will he gain by spending time with children who can hear well?

11. As Jeffrey gets older, what will he gain by spending time with other children with impaired hearing?

Name ______________________ Date ____________ Class ____________

# Study Guide

CHAPTER 26

Managing Life as a Parent

**Directions:** Complete the items that follow in the space provided.

1. Nearly all families experience role conflicts to some degree. What four factors can increase the chances of role conflicts and create family stress?

2. Explain three types of problems that might occur when roles conflict.

3. Describe a balanced life.

4. Why is it important to be realistic in setting priorities?

5. What are some questions parents can ask themselves if their work seems to be interfering with family life?

6. Explain how parents can set boundaries in at least two of the following areas: work, family, personal time, and community involvement.

7. What are the four steps in the management process?

(Continued on next page)

8. Give three examples of how responsibilities might be shared in a family.

9. Offer four examples of household organization.

10. What are two basic time management tools?

11. Give four additional time management tips.

12. How can parents manage stress? Offer four suggestions.

13. Describe how to set up a budget.

14. Give two tips for controlling debt.

15. How can families benefit from a shorter workweek? From telecommuting?

16. What are three sources of support for parents?

Name ______________________ Date ____________ Class ____________



# Overwhelmed? Overcome It

**Directions:** Stacy is a single parent with two children, 9-year-old Laura and 6-year-old Will. She takes a class Monday, Wednesday, and Friday mornings, and she works part-time Monday through Thursday afternoons. One Thursday evening, Stacy is feeling overwhelmed by everything she has to do. She has made a list of what she hopes to accomplish in the next two days. Read Stacey's list below, then complete the items that follow.

**To do Friday and Saturday:**

- Take dog to vet for vaccinations (or schedule appointment)
- Return my mother's phone call (she left a message this afternoon and is out this evening)
- Buy groceries
- Bake homemade lasagna and cookies for Saturday (Laura invited three friends for lunch at 12:30)
- Take Will to his Saturday morning Youth Soccer from 10 to 11 (half an hour away)
- Take children to school Friday and pick them up—it's my turn on car pool duty
- Go to class Friday morning 9:30 to 10:30 (20 minutes away)
- Study for Monday's test—should take two or three hours
- Buy a birthday present for Will to take to his classmate's party on Sunday
- Clean up the mess in the kitchen and bathroom before Laura's friends get here
- Tidy the rest of the rooms they will see
- Call dentist to set up appointments
- Get some exercise
- Get some relaxation
- Fill out forms to apply for a promotion at work
- Do laundry

1. What roles does Stacy have, based on her to-do list?

_______________________________________________

_______________________________________________

2. Which are the highest priority items on Stacy's list?

_______________________________________________

_______________________________________________

3. What could be crossed off the list as unnecessary, if anything?

_______________________________________________

_______________________________________________

4. What could be multi-tasked or dovetailed, if anything?

_______________________________________________

_______________________________________________

(Continued on next page)

## Overwhelmed? Overcome It (continued)

5. Which tasks could Laura and Will do or help with, if any?

______________________________________________

6. What resources from outside the family might help, if any?

______________________________________________

7. Comment on how Stacy is balancing her time between work, school, family, personal activities, and community involvement.

______________________________________________

______________________________________________

______________________________________________

______________________________________________

8. How might Stacy apply the four-step management process to getting ready for Laura's friends?
   a. Plan: ______________________________________________

   ______________________________________________

   b. Organize: ______________________________________________

   ______________________________________________

   c. Implement: ______________________________________________

   ______________________________________________

   d. Evaluate: ______________________________________________

   ______________________________________________

9. Fill out the calendar below to plan Stacy's activities for Friday and Saturday:

| Friday | Saturday |
| --- | --- |
| | |

Name ______________________ Date ______________ Class ______________

# Study Guide

CHAPTER 27

Facing Family Challenges

**Directions:** Complete the items that follow in the space provided.

1. What emotions might parents experience during a family crisis?

2. What stress management techniques are helpful for parents going through a crisis?

3. Name four possible emotional and behavioral effects of a family crisis on children.

4. Offer five guidelines for helping children through a family crisis.

5. How does the information parents communicate with children about a family crisis change with the age of the child?

6. Identify five types of resources available to families during challenging times.

7. How might children feel about moving to a new home?

8. Offer three tips for making moving less stressful for children.

(Continued on next page)

9. Give three guidelines for telling children their parents are divorcing.

10. Name two things parents should *not* do when they are getting a divorce.

11. What is a blended family?

12. What are some adjustments children must make in a blended family? Name at least three.

13. Suggest at least three ways parents can help their children adjust to a blended family.

14. Why should children be included when the family is facing financial difficulties?

15. Give four tips for helping children cope when the family has financial problems.

16. Are drug and alcohol abuse limited to one type of family? Explain.

(Continued on next page)

17. What are some possible effects of parents' drug or alcohol abuse?

18. What can family members do when a parent is abusing drugs or alcohol?

19. What should family members NOT do when a parent is abusing drugs or alcohol?

20. List three signs of substance abuse in children and adolescents.

21. What can substance abuse in children and teens lead to?

22. Describe three steps parents can take when they suspect substance abuse.

23. What is domestic violence?

24. How can parents keep their anger and frustration from leading to family violence?

25. What should an abused family member do in an immediate crisis?

(Continued on next page)

26. In addition to educating children about gangs and the danger they pose, what can parents do to help keep their children safe from gang violence?

27. How can parents help children when a family member has a serious illness?

28. Describe possible ways children may react to the death of a family member.

29. Should children attend a family member's funeral? Why or why not?

30. Give one suggestion each for helping toddlers and preschoolers, school-age children, and adolescents cope with grief.

Name ______________________ Date ______________ Class ______________

CHAPTER 27

Facing Family Challenges

# Moving Time

**Directions:** Imagine that your family plans to move in the middle of August, from your apartment in the big city to a house in a small town 20 miles away. You have an eight-year-old daughter and a five-year-old son. Use your imagination and what you have learned to fill in the items below.

### Getting Ready

1. When will you tell the children about the move? Why did you choose that date?

2. What words might you use to break the news?

3. Your eight-year-old says, "All my friends are here. I don't want to move." What do you say?

4. Your five-year-old says, "Can we come back whenever we want? I like my room." What do you say?

5. What will you do before moving day to help your children begin to feel familiar with the place you are moving to?

### Moving Week

6. What task will you assign the eight-year-old so she can participate in the move?

7. What task will you assign the five-year-old so he can participate in the move?

### After the Move

8. Your eight-year-old says, "I'm bored. I don't know anybody here." What do you say?

9. Your five-year-old acts quiet and sad. What do you say or do?

10. What family activity can you do in your new community to help everybody feel more at home?

Name ______________________ Date ______________ Class ______________

CHAPTER 27

Facing Family Challenges

# Family Changes

**Directions:** Read the following story about the changes in a family. As you read, fill in your suggestions for Sandy, Rod, and Ted.

Sandy and Rod have been having serious problems in their marriage for the last couple of years. After going through counseling, they agree it would be best for Rod to move out of the house. They both expect that this separation will lead to a divorce. They are concerned about how this will affect their seven-year-old daughter.

1. Suggest three things Sandy and Rod might tell their daughter before Rod moves out of the house.

______________________________________________

______________________________________________

______________________________________________

______________________________________________

2. Suggest three ways Sandy and Rod can help their child cope emotionally after Rod has moved out.

______________________________________________

______________________________________________

______________________________________________

______________________________________________

Sandy and Rod go through with the divorce. Sandy is given custody of their daughter. About a year later, Sandy marries Ted, who has a 14-year-old daughter of his own.

3. Suggest two ways Sandy can help her daughter adapt to her new stepfather, Ted.

______________________________________________

______________________________________________

______________________________________________

4. Suggest two ways Sandy can help develop her relationship with her new stepchild, Ted's daughter.

______________________________________________

______________________________________________

______________________________________________

5. Suggest two ways Sandy and Ted can help their children adapt to being stepsiblings.

______________________________________________

______________________________________________

______________________________________________

Name ______________________ Date ______________ Class ______________

# Study Guide

CHAPTER 28

Child Care and Education Options

**Directions:** Complete the items that follow in the space provided.

1. Why do parents choose care or education programs for young children?

2. How does the focus of child care programs differ from that of early childhood education programs?

3. What factors should parents take into consideration when looking for care and education programs for children?

4. Explain three steps for choosing a care or education program.

5. When evaluating the quality of a program, what four factors should parents consider?

6. How can parents manage the cost of child care and education for their children?

7. What are two options for programs for children with special needs?

(Continued on next page)

8. Name three general types of care arrangements for young children. Which offers children the most homelike experience?

9. Who most often provides in-home care?

10. What are three advantages of informal care arrangements in a child's home? What is one drawback?

11. What are three other types of in-home care? Describe each.

12. What is family child care?

13. Name nine areas of regulation for licensing of family child care homes.

14. What are some advantages and drawbacks to child care centers?

15. When evaluating a program, what are two helpful things for parents to look for concerning the following?

The program itself:

The teachers or caregivers:

Health and safety practices:

(Continued on next page)

16. Name five signs that should cause parents to be concerned about a program.

17. What is the difference between licensing and accreditation?

18. Why is a low turnover rate among center staff favorable?

19. Evaluate this center's staff-to-child ratio, according to recommendations: The infant/toddler room has two caregivers and seven children, the room for two-year-olds has three caregivers and ten children, and the preschool room has one caregiver and eight children.

20. List five types of center sponsorship.

21. Offer five tips for easing the separation between parent and child.

22. What are two options for school-age child care?

(Continued on next page)

23. What are four rules a child should learn about staying home alone?

24. What are some backup options for child care when a child is sick or the caregiver facility is unavailable?

25. Name six types of early childhood education programs.

26. In general, how have kindergarten programs changed over the years?

27. What are the three main options for educating school-age children?

28. Describe three advantages and one drawback of home schooling.

29. Name four ways for parents to be involved in their children's program.

30. List three things parents can do to promote children's academic success.

Name ______________________ Date ______________ Class ______________



# Choosing the Best Care

**Part I. Directions:** For each preschool child care option listed below, list an advantage, a disadvantage, two questions a parent should ask before making a decision, and two things to watch for when observing.

**Babysitting cooperative**

Advantage: ______________________

Disadvantage: ______________________

Questions to ask:

1. ______________________
2. ______________________

Things to observe:

1. ______________________
2. ______________________

**Nanny or au pair**

Advantage: ______________________

Disadvantage: ______________________

Questions to ask:

1. ______________________
2. ______________________

Things to observe:

1. ______________________
2. ______________________

**Family child care home**

Advantage: ______________________

Disadvantage: ______________________

______________________

Questions to ask:

1. ______________________
2. ______________________

Things to observe:

1. ______________________
2. ______________________

(Continued on next page)

**Privately owned child care center**

Advantage: ______________________________

Disadvantage: ______________________________

Questions to ask:

1. ______________________________
2. ______________________________

Things to observe:

1. ______________________________
2. ______________________________

**Parent cooperative child care center**

Advantage: ______________________________

Disadvantage: ______________________________

Questions to ask:

1. ______________________________
2. ______________________________

Things to observe:

1. ______________________________
2. ______________________________

**Part II. Directions:** Imagine that you are a young parent who has stayed home with your child for the first two years. Now you want to get a part-time job and want to choose the best child care for your child. Consider the information above and answer the questions below to reach your decision.

What elements of the situation, or context, do you need to consider?

______________________________

______________________________

What is your desired goal?

______________________________

______________________________

Which child care options might work for you?

______________________________

______________________________

What are the possible consequences of those options, including the risks?

______________________________

______________________________

Which option will you choose for your child, and why?

______________________________

______________________________

Name ______________________ Date ____________ Class ____________



# Study Guide

**Directions:** Complete the items that follow in the space provided.

1. Why is career planning important?

2. What four personal qualities should you take into account when deciding on a career?

3. What are career assessment tests? How can they help you?

4. Name four resources for researching potential careers.

5. What five factors should you take into consideration when making your career plan?

6. What level of education would you most likely need for the following career goals?
   Medical assistant: ____________
   Automotive technology: ____________
   Marketing: ____________
   CAD/drafting: ____________

7. What are two ways to gain experience in your field of interest?

8. How can you use the Internet to find job leads?

9. What groups of people might be networking contacts?

(Continued on next page)

10. What information should you include on your résumé?

11. Why should you research a company before you interview there?

12. Offer at least six tips for making a good impression during an interview.

13. Should you accept a job on the spot when one is offered to you? Explain.

14. Name at least five responsible work habits.

15. How can you communicate effectively on the job when speaking, listening, and writing?

16. Name four considerations in making ethical decisions on the job.

17. How can you explain a previous forced job loss at an interview?

18. What are two ways to continue your education after entering the workforce?

Name ______________________ Date ______________ Class ______________



# Applying Your Skills

**Directions:** Imagine having a job in each of the three workplace settings in the table below. Fill in the table to show how you might use each of the basic workplace skills listed in the left column. Consult page 622 of *Parenting: Rewards & Responsibilities* for a more detailed description of each basic skill.

| | Preschool | Pediatrician's Office | Teen Recreation and Counseling Center |
|---|---|---|---|
| Basic Skills | | | |
| Thinking Skills | | | |
| Personal Qualities | | | |
| Resource Management Skills | | | |
| Interpersonal Skills | | | |
| Information Skills | | | |
| Systems Skills | | | |
| Technology Skills | | | |

Name ______________________ Date ____________ Class ____________



# Getting the Job You Want

**Directions:** Imagine you are a young adult who hopes to have a career related to child care. Fill in the items below to show how you would research careers and look for a job. Use another sheet of paper if needed.

1. **Assessing yourself.** Fill in the personal qualities you have (or that the imaginary young adult has) that might relate to a career in child care.
   Your interests: ______________________
   Your abilities: ______________________
   Your values: ______________________
   Your personality: ______________________
2. **Researching careers.** Consult one of the reference sources listed in the chapter or another source.
   Reference consulted: ______________________
   One career suited to someone with the qualities listed above: ______________________
   Brief description of the career: ______________________
   ______________________
3. **Getting ready.** Answer the following questions about the career you chose above.
   What kind of education, training, or experience is required? ______________________
   ______________________
   How long will the preparation take? ______________________
   Would you need to relocate? Explain. ______________________
4. **Finding job opportunities.** Complete the following items.
   Name three ways to find out about jobs: ______________________
   Using one of those resources, identify a specific job opportunity related to the career you chose:
   ______________________
   ______________________
5. **Applying for a job.** Assume you are applying for the job you identified above.
   Name three types of information to include in your resume: ______________________
   ______________________
   Name one purpose of your cover letter: ______________________
   Name two possible references: ______________________
   Name one way to prepare for the interview: ______________________
   What will you do after the interview? ______________________
   Name two things to consider before accepting a job offer: ______________________